Septuagint:

Leviticus

Septuagint, Volume 3

Scriptural Research Institute

Published by Digital Ink Productions, 2025

COPYRIGHT

While every precaution has been taken in the preparation of this book, the publisher assumes no responsibility for errors or omissions, or for damages resulting from the use of the information contained herein.

Septuagint: Leviticus

The Septuagint was translated into Greek at the Library of Alexandria between 250 and 132 BCE.

This English translation was created by the Scriptural Research Institute from 2019 through 2025, primarily from the Codex Vaticanus, although other Septuagint manuscripts were also used for reference. Additionally, the Leningrad Codex, Peshitta, Targums, Vetus Latina manuscripts, and Dead Sea Scrolls were used for comparative analysis.

The image used for the cover is "The Sinai Event" by Raven Mahikan.

TABLE OF CONTENTS

TABLE OF CONTENTS

FORWARD

In the mid-3rd century BCE, King Ptolemy II Philadelphus of Egypt ordered a translation of the ancient Israelite scriptures for the Library of Alexandria, which resulted in the creation of the Septuagint. The original version, published circa 250 BCE, only included the Torah, or in Greek terms, the Pentateuch. The Torah is the five books traditionally credited to Moses, circa 1500 BCE: *Cosmic Genesis, Exodus, Leviticus, Numbers,* and *Deuteronomy.*

The Greek name of the book of Leviticus was *to Leuitikón* (το Λευιτικόν), which translates as "of Levites." The Levites were the priestly tribe of the Israelites, who the book of Leviticus establishes as hereditary priests, with established cities to live in. The Hebrew name of the book is wayyiqrā' (וַיִּקְרָא), normally anglicized as *Vayikrá.* The Hebrew name is based on the first word of the book, which translates as "and he called." The English name is a direct copy of the Old Latin name Leviticus, which shares a common origin with the Greek. This book was not in the *Samareitikon* (Σαμαρειτικὸν), the translation of the Samaritan Torah made at the Library of Alexandria before the Septuagint, and therefore, the book "of Levites" likely seemed like an addition to the Greek translators working at the Library of Alexandria. The Old Latin translators seemed to have viewed the book the same way and named it accordingly.

FORWARD

The textual differences between the Greek *Leviticus* and Hebrew *Vayikrá* are far less significant than the textual differences in the other books of the Torah, supporting the book as having been written quite recently before it was translated into Greek. The laws of the book correlate with the religious reforms of the Judahite king Josiah, who reigned between 640 and 609 BCE. This was less than 400 years before the Greek translation was made. His reforms apparently began with someone finding an "original" copy of Moses' laws in the Temple in Jerusalem, which then became the basis of his official Torah. The laws found in Leviticus parallel his reforms as described in *4th Kingdoms* and Masoretic *Kings*, and therefore the book is generally viewed as originating in his time. This is supported by the fact that neither the Samaritans nor the Egypto-Israelites accepted the book in pre-Hellenic times. The Samaritans continued to use their four-book Torah until the Hasmonean dynasty destroyed all copies in the late-2nd century BCE.

The Egypto-Israelites were mostly descended from Arameans and Samaritans who were driven out of Hama, Damascus, and Samaria as the Neo-Assyrian Empire expanded in the 8th and 7th centuries BCE. They generally did not use a copy of the Torah and did not think much of Moses, which was common among the Aramaean Israelites. While some Israelite literature was translated into Demotic Egyptian and later the Egyptian form of Aramaic, there are no Egypto-Aramaic copies of Leviticus, or even fragments of the book, suggesting it was not used in Egypt.

FORWARD

The only Israelite priesthood that appears to have ever used the book of *Leviticus* was the Judahite priesthood, which explains why there are so few textual differences between the Greek and Hebrew versions. Judahite, the language in which it would have been written, was the Canaanite dialect that Classical Hebrew was based on. The only change to the book that the Hasmonean dynasty appears to have made was to transcribe it into the Aramaic square script, now known as the Hebrew script.

Since the 1800s, the majority of Biblical scholars have interpreted the books of *Leviticus* and *Numbers* as a later addition to the original laws of Moses found in *Exodus*, with *Deuteronomy* being an even later addition during the Babylonian or Persian eras. Cosmic Genesis is either considered to be part of Moses' original work or a later addition in the Persian era, depending on the scholar. *Leviticus* and *Numbers* contain several amendments to Moses' laws in *Exodus*, and established the land rights of the various tribes of Israel within historic Canaan, including the assignment of several cities and their environs to the Levitical Priesthood. The most obvious amendment to Moses' laws is replacing the sacrifice of the firstborn with the establishment of the Levitical Priesthood. *Exodus* chapter 13 includes a requirement that the firstborn Israelites must be slaughtered as a sacrifice to the Lord; however, it allowed an animal to be substituted. This law would not have been difficult for a group of nomadic shepherds to follow, but would have become progressively more difficult as the Israelites became more urbanized in Canaan.

This seems to have resulted in an increase in child sacrifice, which the prophet Jeremiah spoke out against during his lifetime, estimated at between 650 BCE and 570 BCE. The practice was officially banned by King Josiah around 632 BCE after the Levites "found" the "original" Torah of Moses during the refurbishing of Solomon's Temple. As this could not have been Moses' original Torah, as Moses had nothing to do with the Temple of Solomon, it was likely when *Vayikrá* was added to the Torah. The Torah that had been authorized in Hezekiah's time was likely composed of *Bereshít* (*Cosmic Genesis*), *Names* (*Exodus*), and *Numbers*.

This translation restores the name Yahweh to *Leviticus*, although it does not survive in any complete copies of the Septuagint's Leviticus. All complete copies of the *Leviticus* are later Christian editions dating to the 4th century CE or later; however, the oldest fragments of *Leviticus*, from the 1st century BCE, known as Dead Sea Scroll *4QpapLXXLev*[b], include the name spelled in Greek as Iaō (Ιαω), partially surviving in chapter 3, and surviving complete in chapter 4. The Greek transliteration of the Hebrew and Samaritan Yhwh (ايهزر / יהוה) was Ieuō (Ιευω); however, the transliteration of the name as Iaō (Ιαω) was based on the Egypto-Aramaic spelling of Yåw (יאו). This indicates that Dead Sea Scroll 4QpapLXXLev[b] was almost certainly a copy of the Septuagint's Leviticus that had been translated at the Library of Alexandria.

The Masoretic *Book of Daniel* is the only text that was left partially translated into Hebrew, with the remainder in

4

Aramaic, and as such, can be used for comparison between the Aramaic text, which the Septuagint was based on, and the Hebrew translation that later became the Masoretic text. The Aramaic sections of Masoretic Daniel that were not translated into Hebrew maintain the term 'ădōnāy hā'ĕlōhîm (אֲדֹנָי הָאֱלֹהִים), meaning the "Lord of the gods" where the Septuagint has "Lord the god" (Κυριον τον θεον), however, the Hebrew sections have Yəhwâ 'ĕlōhîm (יְהוָה אֱלֹהִים) where the Septuagint has "Lord the god," suggesting the Greek more accurately reflects the Aramaic source texts than the Hebrew translation. According to the Talmud, this was to repair the damage King Manasseh had done 600 years earlier when he removed the name Yahweh from the Israelite texts, however, no evidence has survived from the era of Manasseh or earlier that proves the name was originally in the text, suggesting it was an attempt by the first Hasmonean High-Priest/King Simon the Zealous to create a national Judean religion with a god having a name similar to the Roman god Jupiter (Jove).

In the case of Leviticus, the Greek text generally treats the word "Lord" (Κύριοσ) as a name, unlike in most books of the Septuagint, in which the term was a title, "the Lord" (ὁ κύριοσ), presumably translated from the Aramaic 'ădōnāy (אֲדֹנָי), as still found in the Masoretic Book of Daniel. This treatment of the Lord as a name supports the early-Christian redaction of Yahweh in Leviticus when his name was stripped from the Septuagint, and replaced with "Lord." It is unclear how common the name Yahweh was in the original Greek translation; however, as Leviticus appears to have been written during the lifetime of King Josiah, whose god was Yahweh, it is highly probable that Yahweh would have been mentioned exclusively, and therefore the name is imported from the book of Vayikrá.

The Dead Sea Scrolls support the accuracy of Hebrew transliteration of Vayikrá found in the Leningrad Codex, as the name Yhwh (𐤉𐤄𐤅𐤄) appears in scrolls 4QLev^g and 11QLev^b, in the same places Vayikrá has Yəhwâ (יְהוָה). The book of Leviticus is also the only book in the Torah that is geographically consistent, referring only to Mount Sinai, and never substituting Horeb, Seir, or Hor, as Exodus, Numbers, Deuteronomy, and Judges do. This implies that it was not harmonized from a group of older texts like Numbers, but written more or less as it is. There are still archaic elements within it, such as the repeated references to the horns of the altar; however, as archaeology has discovered that Josiah's god Yahweh was a calf-god, this does make sense in the context of the era.

The book of Vayikrá is also unique in the Torah in not using the word ålhym (אלהים) as a name. The word does survive in some places as part of the phrase hålhym (האלהים), generally accepted as meaning "the god." At one point in chapter 3, "the god" in the Septuagint is mirrored by laYhwâ (לְיהוָה), meaning "the Yhwâ" in the Leningrad Codex. This indicates that the Hasmonean editors were also replacing ålhym with Yahweh. The name ålhym (אלהים), found in other books of the Torah in the Leningrad Codex, is commonly translated as "God," but is a plural form of the

6

Aramaic âlhâ (𐡀𐡋𐡄𐡀), meaning "gods," or a plural form of the Hebrew ēlâ (אֱלָה) meaning "goddesses." The terms âlhym (𐤀𐤋𐤄𐤉𐤌) in Canaanite, and âlhym (𐡌𐡉𐡄𐡋𐡀) in Aramaic, are also direct transcriptions of the Assyrian cuneiform word elium (𒀭𒈨𒍑𒌝), which by the Iron Age meant "god," explaining why the Aramaic term Âlhym (𐡌𐡉𐡄𐡋𐡀) would have been interpreted as "god" by the Greeks.

The term Âlhyn (𐤍𐤉𐤄𐤋𐤀) was also recorded as one of the names of the prophet Balaam in the Deir Alla Inscription (KAI 312), which is accepted as the Moabite spelling of the name. In Aramaic, the name was spelled as both Âlhym (𐡌𐡉𐡄𐡋𐡀) and Âlhyn (𐡍𐡉𐡄𐡋𐡀), confirming that these were viewed as two regional pronunciations of the same name. The Deir Alla Inscription was found in Jordan in 1967, and generally dated to between 880 and 770 BCE. At the time, the region where it was found was part of the country of Moab, and Balaam, the prophet mentioned in Numbers, was an ancient Moabite prophet who was recorded as worshiping several gods, including Âlhyn. This was more than a century before King Josiah's Yahwist reforms; however, it does indicate that Âlhyn was still used as a proper name in southern Canaan at the time, making its absence from Vayikrá conspicuous.

The name Iaō (Ιαω) was removed from the Christian copies of the Septuagint during the 2nd and 3rd century Gnostic-influenced debates over whether Yahweh was the Christian devil or not. The term "Lord" (Κύριοσ) replaced Yahweh during the debates; however, before that, some versions of the Septuagint used Iaō (Ιαω), or the "sacred name" written in either the Aramaic or Phoenician scripts. The copies of the Septuagint that imported the name written in the Aramaic or Phoenician scripts are referred to as kaige revisions, and appear to have originated in Herodian Judea in the 1st century BCE.

According to Origen of Alexandria in the late 2nd century CE, the most accurate name was the Phoenician script version. Theodoret of Cyprus reported in the 5th century that Samaritans pronounced the name as Iabe (Ιαβε) or Iabai (Ιαβαι). Jews substitute the word hšm (השם) in all non-scriptural contexts, which is accepted within rabbinical Judaism as meaning "the name." Christians have traditionally translated it several ways, including Jova, Jehova, and Jehovah, while historians prefer "Yahweh."

As the stories of Abraham, Isaac, and Jacob passing through Canaan all agree that the Canaanites were worshiping the same God as Abraham, this god must have been El, which would have been written as Ān (✳) in Akkadian cuneiform. The lack of any early mention of Yahweh in Bereshít before the Hasmonean redaction also explains the lack of any names ending in -iah before Beriah, who was born in Egypt. Joseph's marriage to the daughter of the High Priest of Iunu (Greek: Heliopolis, Hebrew: Åwn) after interpreting the Pharaoh's dreams implies that he became the High Priest of Iôhw, the lunar god of Heliopolis. The word Iôh (⌒) was the Egyptian word for the moon; however, when treated as a god, it was modified to Iôhw (𓇼𓏏𓇳𓅱), resulting in the two pronunciations of the name Yh (𝕷^) and Yhw (𝕷𝕷^) found in Aramaic.

The earliest depictions of Yahweh, on pottery shards found at Kuntillet Ajrud, dating to circa 800 BCE, depict Yhwh as the calf of Asherah, who was herself the personification of the starry sky, meaning Yahweh was still considered to be the moon at the time.

In chapter 6 of the book of Exodus, God makes a curious statement when he introduces himself to Moses:

> *"I'm Lord, and I appeared to Abraham, Isaac, and Jacob, as their god Ōn, and I did not tell them my name was Lord."*

The Leningrad Codex version reads almost identically:

> *"I'm Yahweh, and I appeared to Abraham, Isaac, and Jacob, as their god Shaddai, and I did not tell them my name was Yahweh."*

This verse was viewed as one of the most obvious places where the name of the lord had been removed from the Torah before it was restored during the Hebrew translation made during the Hasmonean dynasty. The tractate Sanhedrin (103b) in the Talmud reports that King Manasseh was blamed for removing the name; however, as his grandson Josiah "restored" the Torah circa 625 BCE, one would expect that he would have restored the name as well, if it had been in Exodus to begin with. As the Greek translations of Cosmic Genesis, Exodus, and Numbers all include the same discrepancy in comparison to the Leningrad Codex, the missing name Shaddai, this was likely the name that Manasseh removed from the Aramaic translation that had been made during the reign of his father King Hezekiah.

The section of text in Cosmic Genesis dealing with the genealogy of nations appears to have been written in Aramaic, and includes a scribal note that identifies Kalhu as the capital of Assyria, which dates the Aramaic translation to sometime before 706 BCE. Additionally, the presence of the Ashkenaz in the genealogy of nations places the origin of that section of text sometime after 715 BCE, when the Ashkenaz were first documented by the Assyrians, meaning that the Aramaic translation appears to have been made during the rule of King Hezekiah of Judah.

King Hezekiah is recorded in 4th Kingdoms (Masoretic Kings) as initiating a number of reforms to the religion of Judah, including destroying the bamahs which Moses instructed the Israelites to worship at, as well as destroying the statue of the serpent that Moses had made, and which Solomon had erected in the temple in Jerusalem, suggesting that it was Hezekiah who removed the name from the text. If so, the name removed would not have been Yahweh, the god that Hezekiah worshiped, but Shaddai, the god of *Bereshít* (Masoretic *Cosmic Genesis*), *Names* (Masoretic *Exodus*), and Masoretic *Numbers*.

It is generally accepted that there were several versions written in Phoenician and Aramaic before the translation of the Septuagint. Fragments of the Torah have been found in four languages among the Dead Sea Scrolls, generally dated to between 200 BCE and 600 CE. During this time, the land of

Judea passed from the rule of the Ptolemies in Egypt to the rule of the Seleucids in Syria around 200 BCE. The Seleucids attempted to Hellenize the Judeans and effectively banned traditional Judaism.

This Hellenizing activity was partially successful, creating the Sadducee faction of Judaism; however, it also led to the Maccabean Revolt in 165 BCE, which itself created the independent Kingdom of Judea. This Kingdom had a tenuous alliance with the Roman Republic until General Pompey conquered Syria into the Roman Republic in 69 BCE. Pompey's goal was to liberate Greek-speaking communities in the Middle East that had fallen under the rule of non-Greeks when the Seleucid Syrian Empire had collapsed, and he carved up Judea and Edom to the east, placing Greek-speaking cities under the protection of the Roman province of Syria. He also liberated several smaller communities that had been occupied by Judea, granting them self-government, including Ashdod, Yavne, Jaffa, Dora, Marissa, and Samaria.

A series of wars, including both of Julius Caesar's campaigns and a Parthian invasion, led to the weakening of the Hasmonean dynasty, and in 37 CE, the Roman Senate appointed Herod the Great as King of the Jews. Herod's rule wasn't particularly popular, as he allowed the Romans to establish themselves within Judea; however, he did expand Judea, reintegrating the Greek and Samaritan cities, and annexing Galilee and Edom. When he died, his kingdom was divided between four successors, a situation that ended in 66 CE when the Romans conquered the region. An uprising in

120 CE led to the Jews being exiled from Judea, and the region became a Greco-Roman colony. In the wake of the Jews, the Samaritans rose in numbers, along with the Christians, once Christianity was legalized. Between 529 and 555 CE, the Samaritans revolted and were effectively annihilated by the Byzantine Empire.

The ancient documents found in the Caves in Qumran, more commonly called the Dead Sea Scrolls, span a large section of Judean history. The fragments of the Torah have been found in ancient Canaanite, Aramaic, Hebrew, and Greek. The Canaanite fragments in the Dead Sea Scrolls have been particularly debated, as they are believed to be the oldest. The current Hebrew script was officially adopted by the Hasmonean Dynasty in 140 BCE, when the first King / High-Priest Simon the Zealous issued an authoritative Hebrew translation of the Torah. The Hasmonean dynasty paid scribes to replace older versions of the Torah and other non-Hebrew scriptures that were in use, and ordered everyone to bring in their old texts to get the new and improved versions.

The new Hebrew language of Judea was a combination of the old spoken dialect of Canaanite used in the region, which had been written in the Phoenician script, today called Paleo-Hebrew, and the "block letter" version of the Aramaic script. Unfortunately, almost no one in the Kingdom of Judea could read the new Hebrew Torah, and so the Aramaic Targum was also developed to explain what the Hebrew texts said. Before the new Hebrew version was published, there were two versions in circulation in Judea: the Aramaic version used by the Judean intelligentsia, and the Phoenician script Paleo-Hebrew version, which appears to have mainly been used by Samaritans. The Samaritans refused to accept the new Hebrew translation, and so the Hasmoneans slaughtered their priesthood, destroyed their cities, and enslaved the entire Samaritan population, selling most of them to the Egyptians. Eventually, the Roman General Pompey marched through Judea and freed the surviving Samaritans from the Judeans.

The modern Samaritan religion is similar to Judaism in that they have versions of the Torah and the book of Joshua; however, they do not trace their ancestry to ancient Judah, but rather to ancient Samaria, also called the Kingdom of Israel. According to the Samaritans, they were the original Israelites, and the Temple of the Lord was not Solomon's Temple in Jerusalem, but rather a Temple of Mount Gerizim, in Samaria. These other Israelites also contributed to the creation of the Septuagint, as the Book of Tobit was the story of a Samaritan who had been taken to Nineveh, the capital of the Assyrian Empire, after the Kingdom of Israel was conquered by the Assyrians. This book and several others were not considered important to Simon the Zealous and were not translated into Hebrew.

Outside of Judea, the Septuagint was the dominant form of Israelite scriptures across the Greek-speaking world, which at the beginning of the Christian era extended from the Roman Empire in the west to the Indo-Greek Kingdom in the east. Judean traders had established small colonies along the trade routes of the Red Sea and the Indian Ocean, reaching as far south as Eritrea, and as far east as southern India, and these Judeans spoke Aramaic and Greek and used the Septuagint and Targum. The earliest Christians used the Septuagint exclusively, as far as the Israelite scriptures were concerned, and as a result, it is impossible to even understand the chronology of the world they described unless using the Septuagint. It is unclear why the Septuagint, Masoretic Text, and Samaritan Asatir each contain a different chronology of the world. Adding the Book of Jubilees and various variations of the Torah found within the Dead Sea Scrolls, there are no less than six ancient Israelite chronologies.

The Septuagint's *Cosmic Genesis* includes an additional millennium of human history that was dropped from *Bereshít* in order to align the creation of the world with the beginning of the age of El, when the constellation Taurus became the marker of the northern vernal equinox, in 3760 BCE. The Bull El was the dominant God of the Canaanite pantheon until circa 1700 BCE, when Attar the Goat (Aries) and Yam the Sea-Monster (Cetus) fought for domination of the world beneath the sky, ultimately both being replaced by the god of thunder Ba'al Hadad, in the Canaanite Ba'al Cycle. Traditional Jewish interpretations of the timeline within the Masoretic Text, is further hampered the so-called 'missing years' of Rabbinical Time, in which hundreds of years of the Persian Empire are skipped over in order to make the timeline fit into the era since 3760 BCE, a problem Christian chronologists have never had as Christianity developed after the astrology of Babylonian-era Judaism had been forgotten.

The earliest Bibles all used the Septuagint for the Old Testament, if they had one; however, by the 4th century, some Christian scholars were debating whether they should retranslate the Old Testament from the version the Jews were using, and some even suggested using the Samaritan version. Both suggestions were generally dismissed as heretical, as Jesus and the Apostles had quoted from the Septuagint, even though they had access to the Hebrew version then in use. This argument held in the West until the Middle Ages, when Catholic Bibles switched to the Masoretic Texts. In the east, Orthodox Bibles continued to use the Septuagint, as they do today. To the south, the Ethiopian Tewahedo Church continued to use the Septuagint, and across Asia, the Nestorians continued to use the Septuagint. Only in Western Europe were the later Masoretic Text adopted, abandoning the more ancient Septuagint, on the assumption that the Jews had copied their texts more faithfully than the Greeks had translated them. This assumption was carried forward into the Protestant Churches that broke off from the Catholic Church, and therefore almost all Protestant Bibles use the Masoretic texts as the basis of the Old Testament.

Unfortunately, this means that the earliest Christian writings are generally confusing and ignored by Protestants and Catholics. The earliest Christians of the first and second centuries quoted books that are no longer in the Bible, and as such, their writings are not understood. *Septuagint: Leviticus* is the third in a series of 21st century translations aimed at correcting this problem.

FORWARD

One of the problems with academic translations of the Septuagint is the use of unfamiliar names or terms, as the Septuagint was in Greek, and therefore, many names are unrecognizable to modern readers. This project uses the more commonly understood Hebrew-derived names instead of their Greek translations, such as Canaan instead of Chanaan, and Melchizedek instead of Melchisedec. Common modern names are also used instead of either Greek or Hebrew terms when geographical locations are known, such as the archaeological name Uruk instead of the Greek Orech, or the Hebrew Erech, and the archaeological term Sumer instead of Shinar or Senar. While this could be argued as not being a correct academic procedure, it does fulfill the goal of making the translation easy to read and understand.

CHAPTER 1

Moses[1] was again called by Yahweh,[2] and told from the tabernacle of witness, "Speak to the children of Israel, and say to them, 'If any man among you brings gifts to Yahweh, you will bring your gifts of the livestock and the oxen and the sheep. If his gift is a whole burnt offering, he will bring an undamaged male of the herd to the door of the tabernacle of witness. He will bring it as acceptable before Yahweh. He will lay his hand on the head of the burnt offering as a thing acceptable for him, to make atonement for him.

They will kill the calf before Yahweh, and the sons of Aaron the priests will bring the blood, and they will pour the blood around the altar, which is at the doors of the tabernacle of witness. Having flayed the whole burnt offering, they will divide it by its limbs. The sons of Aaron the priests will place fire on the altar and will stack the wood on the fire. The sons of Aaron the priests will pile up the divided parts, and the head, and the fat on the wood on the fire, the wood which is on the altar. They will wash the entrails and the feet in water, and the priests will put all on the altar. It is a burnt offering, a sacrifice, a smell of sweet savor to Yahweh."

"If his gift to Yahweh is a sheep, a lamb, or a kid, for the whole burnt offering, he will bring a male without imperfection. He will lay his hand on its head, and they will kill it by the side of the altar, towards the north before Yahweh, and the sons of Aaron the priests will pour its blood on the altar and around it. They will divide it by its limbs, and its head, and its fat, and the priests will place them on the wood which is on the fire, on the altar. They will wash the entrails and the feet with water, and the priest will bring all the parts and put them on the altar. It is a burnt offering, a sacrifice, a smell of sweet savor to Yahweh.

If he brings his gift, a burnt offering to Yahweh, from the birds, then he will bring his gift of doves or pigeons. The priest will bring it to the altar and will twist off its head, and the priest will put it on the altar and will wring out the blood at the bottom of the altar. He will take away the crop with the feathers, and will throw it out by the altar towards the east to the place of the ashes. He will break it off from the wings and will not separate it, and the priest will put it on the altar on the wood which is on the fire. It is a burnt offering, a sacrifice, a sweet-smelling savor to Yahweh."

CHAPTER 1 NOTES

1 Codex Vaticanus: Mōusēn (ⲘⲱⲨⳤⲏⲚ)

- Codex Alexandrinus: Mōsēn (ⲘⲱⲥⲏⲚ)

- LXX 72: tō Mōsei (ⲧⲟⲟ Ⲙⲟⲟⲥⲓ). Translation: the Moses

- LXX 126: ton Mōusēn (ⲧ⨁ Ⲙⲟⲟⲩⲥⲓ̄ⲱ). Translation: the Moses

- Leningrad Codex: mōšeh (מֹשֶׁה)

- Peshitta: mwšå (ܡܘܫܐ)

- Targum Onkelos: mšê (מֹשֶׁה)

- Targum Jerusalem II: mšê (מֹשֶׁה)

CHAPTER 1

- Targum Jerusalem: mšê (מֹשֶׁה)
- Sahidic manuscript 2006: Mōusēs (Ⲙⲱⲩⲥⲏⲥ)

This verse does not survive in most of the fragments found among the Dead Sea Scrolls; however, the name "Moses" does survive in later verses that have survived among the Dead Sea Scrolls.

- Dead Sea Scroll 6QpaleoLev: mšh (𐤌𐤔𐤄)
- Dead Sea Scroll 4QLev[b]: mšh (משה)
- Dead Sea Scroll 4QLev-Num[a]: mšh (משה)
- Dead Sea Scroll 11QpaleoLev[a]: mšh (𐤌𐤔𐤄)
- Dead Sea Scroll 4QLev[c]: mšh (משה)

It is generally accepted that at some point before the Septuagint was translated, half of Moses' name was redacted from the text. This theory is based on the similarity of the Egyptian term msỉ (𓄟𓋴), meaning "give birth to," or "created by," which was a common element of Egyptian names. Many kings of Egypt were known as the "msỉ" of a god, including Ramses (𓇳𓄟𓋴), Ahmose (𓇋𓄟𓋴), Tuthmose (𓅜𓄟𓋴), Amenmose (𓇏𓄟𓋴), and Ptahmose (𓁰𓄟𓋴𓏏). A theory that has been circulating since at least the time of Josephus in the 1st century CE, is that Moses' original name was Hapymoses, meaning the 'Nile created him.'

If this is the origin of the name, the name of the god that created Moses was likely dropped from the name very early in Israelite history, as there are no known surviving texts with the full name. The latest this is likely to have happened would have been during the Aramaic translation of King Hezekiah; however, it may have happened much earlier.

An alternate interpretation is that the name is complete and is derived from the Egyptian term mw-šảỏ (𓈗𓄜𓈘), meaning

19

'beginning on water,' which is what the princess stated when she found Moses.

2 Codex Vaticanus: KS (κ̄c̄). Translation: lord

- Leningrad Codex: Yəhwâ (יְהוָֽה)
- Peshitta: mryå (ܡܪܝܐ). Translation: master (or lord)
- Targum Onkelos: Yəyā (??). Translation: Yahweh
- Targum Jerusalem II: Yəyā (??). Translation: Yahweh
- Targum Jerusalem: Yəyā (??). Translation: Yahweh
- Sahidic manuscript 2006: joeis (ⲝⲟⲉⲓⲥ). Translation: master

This verse does not survive in most of the Dead Sea Scrolls; however, the name does survive in later sections of Leviticus.

- Dead Sea Scroll 4QpapLXXLev^b (LXX 802): Iaō (ⲓⲁⲱ)
- Dead Sea Scroll 1QpaleoLev: Yhwh (𐤉𐤄𐤅𐤄)
- Dead Sea Scroll 4QLev-Num^a: Yhwh (יהוה)
- Dead Sea Scroll 4QLev^b: Yhwh (יהוה)
- Dead Sea Scroll 4QLev^c: Yhwh (יהוה)
- Dead Sea Scroll 4QLev^d: Yhwh (יהוה)
- Dead Sea Scroll 4QLev^e: Yhwh (יהוה)
- Dead Sea Scroll 11QpaleoLev^a: Yhwh (𐤉𐤄𐤅𐤄)
- Dead Sea Scroll 11QLev^b: Yhwh (𐤉𐤄𐤅𐤄)
- Dead Sea Scroll MasLev^a: Yhwh (יהוה)
- Dead Sea Scroll MasLev^b: Yhwh (יהוה)

The surviving fragments of Leviticus in Septuagint Manuscript 4QpapLXXLev^b from the Hasmonean Dynasty (140 to 37 BCE) render the name as Iaō (ⲓⲁⲱ) in chapters 3 and 4. This transliteration of the name is based on the Egypto-Aramaic Yåw (יאו), and not the Syro-Aramaic Yhw (יהו), Judahite Yhwh (𐤉𐤄𐤅𐤄), or Hebrew Yhwh (יהוה), indicating that Manuscript

4QpapLXXLev^b was translated from an Egypto-Aramaic source, like most of the books that comprised the Septuagint. The Greek version of he name was later imported to Latin as Iaw.

While it cannot be proven at this time that the original Septuagint's translation of Leviticus used the name Iaō, most scholars believe Leviticus was written by the Levites as an amendment to the Laws of Moses found in Exodus, and to cement their claims to the priesthood of Solomon's Temple, which had been overseen by the Sons of Korah since the time of Solomon. These new laws removed human sacrifice entirely, rather than simply allowing a substituted animal, which strongly implies the Israelites were settled in cities by that time, when inherent inequity would have left the poor without the ability to redeem their firstborn.

Child sacrifice was denounced by the Prophet Jeremiah circa 650 BCE, and banned by King Josiah in 4th Kingdoms (Masoretic Kings) circa 628 BCE, meaning Israelites were practicing child sacrifice then, and therefore, Leviticus could not have been an accepted text until after that time. As Yahweh was the god of both Jeremiah and Josiah, Yahweh was likely the original god in the book of Leviticus.

The name was removed from the Christian copies of the Septuagint during the 2nd and 3rd century Christian-Gnostic debates over whether Iaō was the devil or not. According to Theodoret of Cyprus in the 5th century, Samaritans pronounced the name as Iabe (Ιαβε) or Iabae (Ιαβαι). Christians have traditionally translated the name several ways, including Jehovah, Jehova, and Jova.

The two versions of the name, Yh (יה) and Yhwh (יהוה) in Hebrew, or Yh (𐤉𐤄^) and Yhw / Yâw (𐤉𐤀^ / 𐤉𐤄𐤅^) in Aramaic, are almost prophetically identical to the names of the Egyptian lunar-god of Heliopolis: Îôh (☽) and Îôhw (𓇋𓂝𓎛𓇳), which is likely of origin of the twin names found in the Canaanite scriptures, assuming one accepts the historicity of Joseph as the priest of

Heliopolis in Cosmic Genesis, and the Exodus of Moses, Aaron, and the Israelites from Egypt. As Manuscript 4QpapLXXLev^b is the oldest partially surviving copy of the Septuagint's Leviticus, the name is imported from the Leningrad Codex as Yahweh.

CHAPTER 2

"If a mind brings a gift as a sacrifice to Yahweh, his gift will be fine flour, and he will pour oil on it and will put frankincense on it. It is a sacrifice. He will bring it to the priests, the sons of Aaron, and having taken from it a handful of the fine flour with the oil, and all its frankincense, then the priest will put the memorial of it on the altar, it is a sacrifice, an odor of sweet savor to Yahweh. The remainder of the sacrifice will be for Aaron and his sons, the holiest portion from the sacrifices of Yahweh. If he brings as a gift a sacrifice baked from the oven as a gift to Yahweh of fine flour, he will bring unleavened bread kneaded with oil, and unleavened cakes covered in oil."

"If your gift is a sacrifice from a pan, it is fine flour mingled with oil, unleavened offerings. You will break them into fragments and pour oil on them. It is a sacrifice to Yahweh. If your gift is a sacrifice from the stove, it will be made of fine flour with oil. He will offer this sacrifice to Yahweh and will bring it to the priest. The priest will approach the altar and will remove a memorial piece from it, and will place the remainder on the altar. A burnt offering, a smell of sweet savor to Yahweh. That which is left of the sacrifice will be for Aaron and his sons, holiest from the burnt offerings of Yahweh. You will not leaven any sacrifice which you will bring to Yahweh, for as to any leaven or honey, you will not bring it to offer a gift to Yahweh. You will bring them in the way of fruits to Yahweh, but they will not be offered on the altar for a sweet-smelling savor to Yahweh. Every gift of your sacrifice will be seasoned with salt. Omit not the salt of the covenant of Yahweh from your sacrifices, on every gift of yours you will offer salt to Yahweh your god. If you would offer a sacrifice of first-fruits to Yahweh, it will be new grains ground and roasted for Yahweh, so you will bring the sacrifice of the first fruits. You will pour oil on it and place frankincense on it. It is a sacrifice. The priest will offer the memorial taken from the grains with the oil and all its frank-incense. It is a burnt offering to Yahweh."

CHAPTER 3

"If his gift to Yahweh is a peace-offering, if he brings an ox, whether male or female, he will bring it undamaged before Yahweh. He will lay his hands on the head of the sacrifice and will kill it before Yahweh, by the doors of the tabernacle of witness. The priests, the sons of Aaron, will pour the blood on the altar of burnt offerings around it. They will bring of the peace-offering a burnt sacrifice to Yahweh, the fat covering the belly, and all the fat on the belly. The two kidneys and the fat that is on them. He will take away that which is on the thighs, and the caul above the liver, together with the kidneys. The priests, the sons of Aaron, will offer them on the altar on the burnt offering, on the wood which is on the fire on the altar: it is a burnt offering, a smell of sweet savor to Yahweh. If his gift is from the sheep, a peace-offering to Yahweh, male or female, he will bring it undamaged."

"If he brings a lamb for his gift, he will bring it before Yahweh. He will lay his hands on the head of his offering and kill it by the doors of the tabernacle of witness, and the priests, the sons of Aaron, will pour out the blood on the altar and around it. He will bring the peace-offering, a burnt sacrifice to God.[1] The fat and the hind part he will take away with the loins undamaged, and having taken away all the fat that covers the belly, and all the fat that is on the belly, and both the kidneys and the fat that is on them, and that which is on the thighs, and the caul which is on the liver with the kidneys, the priest will offer these on the altar. It is a sacrifice of sweet savor, a burnt offering to Yahweh."

"If his offering is from the goats, then he will bring it before Yahweh, and he will lay his hands on its head, and they will kill it before Yahweh by the doors of the tabernacle of witness, and the priests, the sons of Aaron, will pour out the blood on the altar and around it. He will offer it as a burnt offering to Yahweh, including the fat that covers the belly, and all the fat that is on the belly. Both the kidneys and all the fat that is on them, that which is on the thighs, and the caul of the liver with the kidneys, will he take away. The priest will offer it on the altar. It is a burnt offering, a smell of sweet savor to Yahweh. All the fat belongs to Yahweh. It is a perpetual statute throughout your generations, in all your habitations. You will eat no fat and no blood."

CHAPTER 3 NOTES

1 Codex Vaticanus: tō Ṯō (ⲦⲰⲐⲰ̄). Translation: the god

• Leningrad Codex: laYhwâ (לַיהוָֹה). Translation: to (or for) Yahweh

• Peshitta: lmryå (ܠܡܪܝܐ). Translation: to (or for, of) master (or lord)

• Targum Onkelos: qŏdām Yəyā (יְיָ קֳדָם). Translation: before (or "in front of") Yahweh

• Targum Jerusalem: qŏdām Yəyā (יְיָ קֳדָם). Translation: before (or "in front of") Yahweh

• Sahidic manuscript 2006: pjoeis (ⲡϫⲟⲉⲓⲥ). Translation: master

Based on the deviation between the Greek and Hebrew translations, it seems likely that the Judahite original read hålhym (𐤀𐤋𐤄𐤉𐤌), meaning 'the ålhym.' The phrase remains in some of the later chapters of Leviticus, where it is mirrored by 'god' in Greek. This suggests that the Hebrew translators were substituting lyhwh (ליהוה) for hålhym and not just 'the lord'.

CHAPTER 4

Yahweh said to Moses, "Say to the children of Israel, 'If a mind will sin unwillingly before Yahweh, in any of the commandments of Yahweh concerning things which he should not do, and does some of them or if the anointed priest sin causes the people to sin, then he will bring for his sin, which he has sinned, an undamaged calf of the herd to Yahweh for his sin.'"

"'He will bring the calf to the door of the tabernacle of witness before Yahweh, and he will put his hand on the head of the calf before Yahweh and will kill the calf in the presence of Yahweh. The anointed priest who has been consecrated, having received the blood of the calf, will then bring it into the tabernacle of witness. The priest will dip his finger into the blood, and sprinkle the blood seven times before Yahweh, over against the holy veil. The priest will put of the blood of the calf on the horns of the altar of the compound incense which is before Yahweh, which is in the tabernacle of witness, and all the blood of the calf will he pour out by the foot of the altar of whole burnt offerings, which is by the doors of the tabernacle of witness, and all the fat of the calf of the sin-offering will he take off from it; the fat that covers the insides, and all the fat that is on the insides, and the two kidneys, and the fat that is on them, which is on the thighs, and the caul that is on the liver with the kidneys, them will he take away, as he takes it away from the calf of the sacrifice of peace-offering, so will the priest offer it on the altar of burnt offering. They will take the skin of the calf, and all his flesh with the head and the extremities and the belly and the dung, and they will carry out the whole calf from the camp into a clean place, where they pour out the ashes, and they will burn it with fire there on wood. It will be burnt on the ashes poured out.'"

"If the whole congregation of Israel ignorantly trespasses, and it should escape the notice of the congregation, and they should do something forbidden in any of the commands of Yahweh, which should not be done, and should transgress, and the sin in which they have sinned should become known to them, then will the congregation bring an undamaged calf of the herd for a sin-offering, and they will bring it to the doors of the tabernacle of witness. The elders of the congregation will lay their hands on the head of the calf before Yahweh, and they will kill the calf before Yahweh. The anointed priest will bring in some of the blood of the calf into the tabernacle of witness. The priest will dip his finger into some of the blood of the calf and will sprinkle it seven times before Yahweh, in front of the veil of the sanctuary. The priest will put some of the blood on the horns of the altar of the incense of composition, which is before Yahweh, which is in the tabernacle of witness, and he will pour out all the blood at the bottom of the altar of whole burnt offerings, which is by the door of the tabernacle of witness. He will take away all the fat from it and will offer it up on the altar. He will do to the calf as he did to the calf of the sin-offering, so will it be done, and the priest will make atonement for them, and the trespass will be forgiven them. They will carry out the calf whole throughout the camp, and they will burn the calf as they burnt the previous calf. It is the sin-offering of the congregation.'"

"'If a ruler sins, and breaks one of the commands of Yahweh his god, doing the thing which should not be done, unwillingly, and will sin and trespass, and his trespass in which he has sinned, becomes known to him, then will he offer for his gift a kid of the goats, a male without imperfection. He will lay his hand on the head of the kid, and they will kill it in the place where they kill the victims for whole burnt offerings before Yahweh. It is a sin-offering. The priest will smear with his finger some of the blood of the sin-offering onto the horns of the altar of the whole burnt offering, and he will pour out all its blood at the bottom of the altar of whole burnt offerings. He will offer up all his fat on the altar, as the fat of the sacrifice of peace-offering, and the priest will make atonement for him concerning his sin, and it will be forgiven him.'"

"'If a mind of the people of the land should sin unwillingly, in doing a thing contrary to any of the commandments of Yahweh, and his sin should become known to him, then he will bring a kid of the goats, a female without imperfection, he will bring for his sin, which he has sinned. He will lay his hand on the head of his sin-offering, and they will kill the kid of the sin-offering in the place where they kill the victims for whole burnt offerings. The priest will take its blood with his finger, and will smear it on the horns of the altar of whole burnt offerings, and all its blood he will pour out at the foot of the altar. He will take away all the fat, like the fat is taken away from the sacrifice of peace-offering, and the priest will offer it on the altar for a smell of sweet savor to Yahweh, and the priest will make atonement for him, and his sin will be forgiven him. If he should offer a lamb for his sin-offering, he will offer a female without imperfection. He will lay his hand on the head of the sin-offerings, and they will kill it in the place where they kill the whole burnt offerings. The priest will take the blood of the sin-offering with his finger, and will put it on the horns of the altar of whole burnt offerings, and he will pour out all its blood at the bottom of the altar of whole burnt offerings. He will take away all his fat, as the fat of the lamb of the sacrifice of peace-offering is taken away, and the priest will put it on the altar for a whole burnt offering to Yahweh,[1] and the priest will make atonement for him for the sin which he sinned, and it will be forgiven him.'"

CHAPTER 4 NOTES

1 Dead Sea Scroll 4QpapLXXLev[b]: Iaō (ιᴀᴄᴜ)

- Codex Vaticanus: ĸs (κ̄ϲ̄). Translation: lord

- Leningrad Codex: Yəhwâ (יְהוָֹה)

- Peshitta: mryå (ܡܪܝܐ). Translation: master (or lord)

- Targum Onkelos: Yəyā (?ּ?). Translation: Yahweh

- Targum Jerusalem II: Yəyā (?ּ?). Translation: Yahweh

- Targum Jerusalem: Yəyā (?ּ?). Translation: Yahweh

CHAPTER 4

• Sahidic manuscript 2006: joeis (ⲭⲟⲉⲓⲥ). Translation: master

The surviving fragments of Leviticus in Septuagint Manuscript 4QpapLXXLev[b] from the Hasmonean Dynasty (140 to 37 BCE) render the name as Iaō (Ιαω) in chapters 3 and 4. This transliteration of the name is based on the Egypto-Aramaic Yåw (𐡉𐡅^), and not the Syro-Aramaic Yhw (𐡉𐡐^), Judahite Yhwh (𐤉𐤄𐤅𐤄), or Hebrew Yhwh (יהוה), indicating that 4QpapLXXLev[b] was translated from an Egypto-Aramaic source, like most of the books that comprised the Septuagint. The Greek version of he name was later imported to Latin as Iaw.

While it cannot be proven at this time that the original Septuagint's translation of Leviticus used the name Iaō, most scholars believe Leviticus was written by the Levites as an amendment to the Laws of Moses found in Exodus, and to cement their claims to the priesthood of Solomon's Temple, which had been overseen by the Sons of Korah since the time of Solomon. These new laws removed human sacrifice entirely, rather than simply allowing a substituted animal, which strongly implies the Israelites were settled in cities by that time, when inherent inequity would have left the poor without the ability to redeem their firstborn.

Child sacrifice was denounced by the prophet Jeremiah circa 650 BCE, and banned by King Josiah in 4th Kingdoms (Masoretic Kings) circa 628 BCE, meaning Israelites were practicing child sacrifice then, and therefore, Leviticus could not have been an accepted text until after that time. As Yahweh was the god of both Jeremiah and Josiah, Yahweh was likely the original god in the book of Leviticus.

The name was removed from the Christian copies of the Septuagint during the 2nd and 3rd century Christian-Gnostic debates over whether Iaō was the devil or not. According to Theodoret of Cyprus in the 5th century, Samaritans pronounced the name as Iabe

(Ιαβε) or Iabae (Ιαβαι). Christians have traditionally translated the name several ways, including Jehovah, Jehova, and Jova.

The two versions of the name, Yh (יה) and Yhwh (יהוה) in Hebrew, or Yh (𐤉𐤄^) and Yhw / Yâw (𐤉𐤅^ / 𐤉𐤄^) in Aramaic, are almost prophetically identical to the names of the Egyptian lunar-god of Heliopolis: Ỉȯḥ (☾) and Ỉȯḥw (𓇼𓎛𓏲𓇳), which is likely of origin of the twin names found in the Canaanite scriptures, assuming one accepts the historicity of Joseph as the priest of Heliopolis in Cosmic Genesis, and the exodus of Moses, Aaron, and the Israelites from Egypt.

As 4QpapLXXLev[b] is the oldest partially surviving copy of the Septuagint's Leviticus, the name is imported from the Leningrad Codex as Yahweh.

CHAPTER 5

"'If a mind[1] sins and hears the voice of swearing, and he is a witness or has seen or been conscious of it, and he does not report it, he will bear his iniquity. That mind which will touch any unclean thing, or carcass, or that which is unclean being taken of animals, or the dead bodies of abominable reptiles which are unclean, or carcasses of unclean livestock, or should touch the uncleanness of a man, or whatever kind, which he may touch and be defiled by, and it should have escaped him, but afterward, he should know, then he has transgressed. That unrighteous mind, which determines with his lips to do evil or to do good according to whatever a man may determine with an oath, and it has escaped his notice, and he will afterward know it, and so he should sin in any one of these things, then will he declare his sin in the things in which he has sinned by that sin. He will bring for his transgressions against Yahweh, for his sin which he has sinned, a ewe lamb of the flock, or a kid of the goats, for a sin-offering, and the priest will make an atonement for him for his sin which he has sinned, and his sin will be forgiven him.'"

"If he can't afford a sheep, he will bring for his sin which he has sinned, two turtledoves or two young pigeons to Yahweh, one for a sin-offering, and the other for a burnt offering. He will bring them to the priest, and the priest will bring the sin-offering first, and the priest will pinch off the head from the neck, and will not divide the body. He will

35

sprinkle of the blood of the sin-offering on the side of the altar, but the rest of the blood he will drop at the foot of the altar, for it is a sin-offering. He will make the second a whole burnt offering, as it is fit, and the priest will make atonement for his sin, which he has sinned, and it will be forgiven him. If he can't afford a pair of turtledoves or two young pigeons, then he will bring as his gift for his sin, a tenth of a bushel of fine flour for a sin-offering; he will not pour oil on it, nor will he put frankincense on it, because it is a sin-offering. He will bring it to the priest, and the priest, having taken a handful of it, will lay the memorial of it on the altar of whole burnt offerings to Yahweh, it is a sin-offering. The priest will make atonement for him for his sin, which he has sinned in one of these things, and it will be forgiven him, and that which is left will be the priest's, as an offering of fine flour.'"

Yahweh said to Moses, "The mind which will be really unaware and will sin unwillingly in any of the holy things of Yahweh, will also bring to Yahweh for his transgression a ram from the flock without imperfection, valued according to shekels of silver according to the shekel of the sanctuary, for his transgression in which he transgressed. He will make compensation for that in which he has sinned in the holy things, and he will add the fifth part to it, and give it to the priest, and the priest will make atonement for him with the ram of transgression, and his sin will be forgiven. The mind which will sin, and do one thing against any of the commandments of Yahweh, which it is not right to do, and has not known it, and has transgressed, and has contracted guilt, he will even bring a ram without imperfection from the flock,

CHAPTER 5

valued at a price of silver for his transgression to the priest, and the priest will make atonement for his trespass of ignorance, in which he ignorantly trespassed, and he did not know it, and it will be forgiven. For he has surely been guilty of transgression before Yahweh."

CHAPTER 5 NOTES

1 Codex Vaticanus: ṡukhē (✝Υ✕Ⱨ). Translation: psyche (or personality, mind)

- Leningrad Codex: nepeš (נֶפֶשׁ). Translation: mind (or person)

- Peshitta: npšå (ܢܦܫܐ). Translation: mind (or person)

- Targum Onkelos: 'ĕnaš (אֱנַשׁ). Translation: human

- Targum Jerusalem: bar naš (בַּר נַשׁ). Translation: son of human

- Sahidic manuscript 2006: ṡuǩē (ⲯⲩⲭⲏ). Translation: life force (psyche, or soul)

CHAPTER 6

Yahweh said to Moses, "The mind which has sinned, and intentionally ignored the commandments of Yahweh, and has dealt falsely in the affairs of his neighbor in the matter of a deposit, or concerning fellowship, or concerning plunder, or has in anything wronged his neighbor, or has found that which was lost, and has lied about it, and has sworn dishonestly concerning anyone regarding anything, whatever a man does to sin, it will come to pass, whenever he has sinned, and transgressed, that he will restore the plunder which he has seized, or redress the injury which he has committed, or restore the deposit which was entrusted to him, or the lost article which he has found of any kind, about which he swore dishonestly, he will even restore it in full, and he will add to it the fifth part besides. He will restore it to him whose it is on the day on which he happens to be convicted. He will bring to Yahweh for his trespass, a ram of the flock, without imperfection, of value to the amount of the thing in which he trespassed. The priest will make atonement for him before Yahweh, and he will be forgiven for all the things which he did and trespassed in it."

Yahweh said to Moses, "Tell Aaron and his sons, 'This is the law of the whole burnt offering. This is the whole burnt offering, which will burn on the altar all night until the morning, and the fire of the altar will burn it, and it will not be put out. The priest will put on the linen tunic, and he will put the linen trousers on his body and will take away that which has been thoroughly burnt, which the fire has consumed, including the whole burnt offering from the altar, and he will put it near the altar. He will take off his robe, and put on another robe, and he will take out the offering that has been burnt out of the camp into a clean place. The fire on the altar will be kept burning on it, and will not be extinguished, and the priest will burn on it wood every morning, and will heap on it the whole burnt offering, and will lay on it the fat of the peace-offering. The fire will always burn on the altar. It will not be extinguished.'"

"'This is the law of the sacrifice, which the sons of Aaron will bring before Yahweh and the altar. He will take from it a handful of the fine flour of the sacrifice with its oil, and with all its frankincense, which are on the sacrifice, and he will offer up on the altar a burnt offering as a sweet-smelling savor, a memorial to Yahweh. Aaron and his sons will eat what is left of it. It will be eaten outside of the holy place; they will eat it in the court of the tabernacle of witness. It will not be baked with leaven. I have given it to them, as a portion of the burnt offerings of Yahweh. It is holiest, as the offering for sin, and as the offering for trespass. Every male of the priests will eat it. It is a perpetual ordinance throughout your generations for the burnt offerings of Yahweh. Whoever will touch them will be sacred.'"

Yahweh said to Moses, "This is the gift for Aaron and his sons, which they will offer to Yahweh in the day in which you will anoint him: a tenth of a bushel of fine flour for a sacrifice continually, half of it in the morning, and half of it in the evening. It will be made with oil in a frying pan. He will offer it kneaded and in rolls, an offering of fragments, an offering of a sweet savor to Yahweh. The anointed priest who is in his place, one of his sons, will offer it. It is a perpetual statute; it will all be consumed. Every sacrifice of a priest will be thoroughly burnt, and will not be eaten."

Yahweh said to Moses, "Tell Aaron and his sons, 'This is the law of the sin-offering: In the place where they kill the whole burnt offering, they will kill the sin-offerings before Yahweh: they are holiest. The priest who offers it will eat it. It will be eaten in a holy place, in the court of the tabernacle of witness. Everyone who touches the flesh will be holy, and on whoever's garment any of its blood has been sprinkled, whoever has it sprinkled, will be washed in the holy place. The earthen vessel, in whichever it has been dirtied, will be broken, and if it has been dirtied in a brazen vessel, he will scour it and wash it with water. Every male priest will eat it. It is holiest to Yahweh. No offerings for sin, of whose blood there will be brought any into the tabernacle of witness to make atonement in the holy place, will be eaten: they will be burnt with fire.'"

"'This is the law of the ram for the trespass-offering. It is sacred. In the place where they kill the whole burnt offering, they will kill the ram of the trespass-offering before Yahweh, and he will pour out the blood at the bottom of the altar and around it. He will offer all the fat from it, and the loins, and all the fat that covers the insides, and all the fat that is on the

insides, and the two kidneys, and the fat that is on them, that
which is on the thighs, and the caul on the liver with the
kidney, he will take them away. The priest will offer them
on the altar a burnt offering to Yahweh, it is for trespass.
Every male of the priest will eat them, in the holy place they
will eat them: they are sacred. Like the sin-offering, so also is
the trespass-offering. There is one law for them; the priest
who will make the atonement with it, it will be his. As for
the priest who offers a man's whole burnt offering, the skin of
the whole burnt offering that he offers will be his. Every
sacrifice which will be prepared in the oven, and every
offering which will be prepared on the stove, or in a frying-
pan, is the property of the priest that offers it. It will be his.
Every sacrifice made up with oil, or not made up with oil,
will belong to the sons of Aaron, an equal portion to each.'"

CHAPTER 7

"This is the law of the sacrificial peace-offering, which they will bring to Yahweh. If a man wants to offer it for praise, then he will bring for the sacrifice of praise, loaves of fine flour made up with oil, and unleavened cakes coated with oil, and fine flour kneaded with oil. With leavened bread, he will offer his gifts, with the peace-offering of praise. He will bring one of all his gifts, a separate offering to Yahweh: it will belong to the priest who pours out the blood of the peace-offering. The flesh of the sacrifice of the peace-offering of praise will be his, and it will be eaten in the day which it is offered: they will not leave it until the morning. If it is a vow, or he offers his gift by his own will, on whatever day he will offer his sacrifice, it will be eaten, and in the morning, that which is left of the flesh of the sacrifice until the third day will be consumed with fire."

"If he does at all eat of the flesh on the third day, it will not be accepted for him that offering. It will not be considered by him; it is pollution, and whatever mind will eat it, will bear his iniquity. Whatever flesh has touched anything unclean, it will not be eaten. It will be burned with fire. Everyone who is clean will eat the flesh. Whatever mind will eat of the flesh of the sacrifice of the peace-offering which is Yahweh's and become unclean, that mind will perish from his people. Whatever mind will touch anything unclean, either of the uncleanness of a man, or unclean quadrupeds, or any unclean abominable thing, and will eat of the flesh of the sacrifice of the peace-offering, which is Yahweh's, that mind will perish from his people."

Yahweh said to Moses, "Tell the children of Israel, 'You will eat no fat of oxen or sheep or goats. The fat of animals that have died by themselves, or have been killed by animals, may be employed for any work, but it will not be eaten for food. Everyone who eats the fat of the animals, from which he will bring a burnt offering to Yahweh, that mind will perish from his people. You will eat no blood in all your houses, either of animals or birds. Every mind that will eat blood, that mind will perish from his people.'"

Yahweh said to Moses, "You will also tell the children of Israel, 'He who offers a sacrifice of peace-offering, will bring his gift to Yahweh also from the sacrifice of peace-offering. His hands will bring the burnt offerings to Yahweh, the fat which is on the breast and the fat from the liver, he will bring them, to set them as a gift before Yahweh. The priest will offer the fat on the altar, and the breast will be Aaron's and his sons, and you will give the right shoulder as a choice piece to the priest of your sacrificial peace-offering. He that offers the blood of the peace-offering, and the fat, of the sons of Aaron, his will be the right shoulder for a portion. For I have taken the wave-breast and shoulder of separation from the children of Israel from your sacrificial peace-offerings, and I have given them to Aaron the priest and his sons, a perpetual ordinance due from the children of Israel. This is the anointing of Aaron, and the anointing of his sons, their portion of the burnt offerings of Yahweh, in the day in which he brought them forward to minister as priests to Yahweh, as Yahweh commanded to give to them in the day in which he anointed them of the sons of Israel, a perpetual statute through their generations.'"

This is the law of the whole burnt offerings, and sacrifice, and sin-offering, and offering for transgression, and the sacrifice of consecration, and the sacrifice of peace-offering, as Yahweh commanded Moses on Mount Sinai, on the day when he commanded the children of Israel to offer their gifts before Yahweh in the Wilderness of Sinai.

CHAPTER 8

Yahweh said to Moses, "Take Aaron and his sons, and his robes and the anointing oil, and the calf for the sin-offering, and the two rams, and the basket of unleavened bread, and assemble the whole congregation at the entrance of the tabernacle of witness."

Moses did as Yahweh appointed him, and he assembled the congregation at the door of the tabernacle of witness. Moses said to the congregation, "This is what Yahweh has commanded you to do."

Moses brought near Aaron and his sons, and washed them with water, and put on him the coat, and girded him with the girdle, and clothed him with the tunic, and put on him the vest, and dressed him in a girdle according to the make of the vest, and clasped him closely with it: and put on it the oracle, the Manifestation and the Truth. He put the miter on his head, with the golden plate in the front, the holiest thing, as Yahweh commanded Moses. Moses took the anointing oil, and sprinkled it seven times on the altar, and anointed the altar, and hallowed it, and all things on it, and the layer, and its foot, and sanctified them, and anointed the tabernacle and all its furniture, and hallowed it. Moses poured the anointing oil on the head of Aaron, and he anointed him and sanctified him.

Moses brought the sons of Aaron near, and put on them coats and girded them with girdles, and put turbans on them as Yahweh commanded Moses. Moses brought near the calf for the sin-offering, and Aaron and his sons laid their hands on the head of the calf of the sin-offering. He killed it, and Moses took of the blood and put it on the horns of the altar round about with his finger, and he purified the altar, and poured out the blood at the bottom of the altar, and sanctified it, to make atonement on it. Moses took all the fat that was on the insides, and the lobe on the liver, and both the kidneys, and the fat that was on them, and Moses offered them on the altar. But the calf's hide, flesh, and dung, he burnt with fire outside the camp, as Yahweh commanded Moses. Moses brought near the ram for a whole burnt offering, and Aaron and his sons laid their hands on the head of the ram. Moses killed the ram, and Moses poured the blood on the altar and around it. He divided the ram by its limbs, and Moses offered the head, the limbs, and the fat, and he washed the belly and the feet with water. Moses offered up the whole ram on the altar. It is a whole burnt offering for a sweet-smelling savor, it is a burnt offering to Yahweh, as Yahweh commanded Moses.

Moses brought the second ram, the ram of consecration, and Aaron and his sons laid their hands on the head of the ram, and he killed him. Moses took some of his blood and put it on the tip of Aaron's right ear, the thumb of his right hand, and the big toe of his right foot. Moses brought near the sons of Aaron, and Moses put of the blood the tips of their right ears, and on the thumbs of their right hands, and the big toes of their right feet, and Moses poured out the blood on the altar and around it. He took the fat, and the rump, and the fat on the belly, and the liver, and the two kidneys, and the fat that

is on them, and the right shoulder. From the basket of consecration, which was before Yahweh, he also took one
unleavened loaf, and one loaf made with oil, and one cake, and
put them on the fat, and the right shoulder, and put them all
in the hands of Aaron, and in the hands of his sons, and offered
them up as an offering before Yahweh.

Moses took them in their hands, and Moses offered them on
the altar, on the whole burnt offering of consecration, which is
a smell of sweet savor. It is a burnt offering to Yahweh. Moses
took the breast, and separated it for a heave-offering before
Yahweh, from the ram of consecration, and it became Moses'
portion, as Yahweh commanded Moses. Moses took the
anointing oil, and of the blood that was on the altar, and
sprinkled it on Aaron, and his garments, and his sons, and the
garments of his sons with him. He sanctified Aaron and his
garments, and his sons, and the garments of his sons with him.

Moses said to Aaron and his sons, "Boil the flesh in the tent
of the tabernacle of witness in the holy place, and there you
will eat it and the loaves in the basket of consecration, as it has
been ordered to me, Yahweh said, 'Aaron and his sons will eat
them.' That which is left of the flesh and of the loaves burn
with fire. You will not go out from the door of the tabernacle
of witness for seven days until the end of the day, the day of
your consecration. For in seven days will he consecrate you,
as he did in this day on which Yahweh commanded me to do
so, to make an atonement for you. You will remain seven
days at the door of the tabernacle of witness, day and night.

CHAPTER 8

You will observe the ordinances of Yahweh, so you don't die. This has been commanded to me by the lord of the gods."[1]

Aaron and his sons performed all these commands that Yahweh had commanded Moses.

CHAPTER 8 NOTES

1 Codex Vaticanus: $\overline{\text{KS}}$ o $\overline{\text{TS}}$ (ⲔⲤⲞⲐⲤ). Translation: Lord the god

• Codex Colberto-Sarravianus: $\overline{\text{KS}}$ (ⲔⲤ). Translation: Lord

• Leningrad Codex: Yəhōwâ (יְהוָה)

• Peshitta: mryå (ܡܪܝܐ). Translation: master

• Targum Onkelos: mərā' daYyā (מְרָא דַיְיָ). Translation: master (or lord) of Yahweh

• Targum Jerusalem: mərā' daYyā (מְרָא דַיְיָ). Translation: master (or lord) of Yahweh

• Sahidic manuscript 2006: joeis (ϫⲟⲉⲓⲥ). Translation: master

CHAPTER 9

It happened on the eighth day that Moses called Aaron and his sons, and the elders of Israel.

Moses said to Aaron, "Take for yourself a young calf of the herd for a sin-offering, and a ram for a whole burnt offering, undamaged, and offer them before Yahweh. Say to the elders of Israel, 'Take one kid of the goats for a sin-offering, and a young calf, and a spotless lamb a year old for a whole burnt offering, and a calf and a ram for a peace offering before Yahweh, and fine flour mixed with oil, for today Yahweh will appear among you.'"

They took what Moses commanded them before the tabernacle of witness, and all the congregation drew near, and they stood before Yahweh. Moses declared, "This is what Yahweh has said. Do it, and the glory of Yahweh will appear among you."

Moses said to Aaron, "Approach the altar, and offer your sin-offering, and your whole burnt offering, and make atonement for yourself, and your house, and offer the gifts of the people, and make atonement for them, as Yahweh commanded Moses."

Aaron approached the altar and killed the calf of his sin-offering. The sons of Aaron brought the blood to him, and he dipped his finger into the blood and put it on the horns of the altar, and he poured out the blood at the bottom of the altar.

CHAPTER 9

He offered up on the altar the fat and the kidneys and the liver of the sin-offering, as Yahweh had commanded Moses. The flesh and the hide he burnt with fire outside the camp. He killed the whole burnt offering, and the sons of Aaron brought the blood to him, and he poured it on the altar and around it. They brought the whole burnt offering, in its pieces. He put them and the head on the altar. He washed the belly and the feet with water, and he put them on the whole burnt offering on the altar.

He took the gift of the people, and took the goat of the sin-offering from the people, and killed it, and purified it also like the first. He brought the whole burnt offering and offered it in the same way. He brought the sacrifice and filled his hands with it, and laid it on the altar, besides the morning whole burnt offering. He killed the calf, and the ram of the sacrifice of peace-offering of the people, and the sons of Aaron brought the blood to him, and he poured it out on the altar and around it. He took the fat of the calf, and the hindquarters of the ram, and the fat covering the belly, and the two kidneys, and the fat on them, and the caul on the liver. He put the fat on the breasts and offered the fat on the altar.

Aaron separated the breast and the right shoulder as a choice-offering before Yahweh, as Yahweh commanded Moses. Aaron lifted his hands over the people and blessed them, and after he had offered the sin-offering, the whole burnt offerings, and the peace-offerings, he came down. Moses and Aaron entered into the tabernacle of witness, and they came out and blessed all the people, and the glory of Yahweh appeared to all the people. Fire came out from Yahweh and devoured the offerings on the altar, both the whole burnt offerings and the fat, and all the people saw, and were amazed, and fell on their faces.

CHAPTER 10

Aaron's two sons, Nadab and Abihu, each took his censer, and put fire in it, and threw incense on it, and offered strange fire before Yahweh, which Yahweh did not command them, and fire came out from Yahweh, and devoured them, and they died before Yahweh.

Moses said to Aaron, "This is what Yahweh said, 'I will be sanctified by those that draw near to me, and I will be glorified in the whole congregation," and Aaron was hurt in his heart.

Moses called Misadae and Elizaphan, the sons of Uzziel, the sons of the brother of Aaron's father, and said to them, "Approach and take your brothers from before the sanctuary out of the camp."

They approached and carried them in their coats out of the camp, as Moses had said.

Moses said to Aaron, and his remaining sons Eleazar and Ithamar, "'You will not shave your heads, and you will not tear your clothes, or you may die, and then there would be anger on all the congregation, and your brothers, even all the house of Israel, would be saddened by the burning, that they were burnt by Yahweh. You will not go out from the door of the tabernacle of witness, that you do not die, for Yahweh's anointing oil is on you."

CHAPTER 10

They did according to the word of Moses.

Yahweh said to Aaron, "Whenever you enter into the tabernacle of witness or when you approach the altar, you will not drink wine or strong drink, you or your sons with you, so you will not die. It is a perpetual statute for your generations, to distinguish between sacred and profane, and between clean and unclean, and to teach the children of Israel all the commandments, which Yahweh spoke to them by Moses."

Moses said to Aaron and his surviving sons Eleazar and Ithamar, 'Take the sacrifice that is left of the burnt offerings of Yahweh, and you will eat unleavened bread by the altar. It is sacred. You will eat it in the holy place, for this is a statute for you and a statute for your sons, of the burnt offerings to Yahweh, for so it has been commanded to me. You will eat the breast of separation, and the shoulder of the choice-offering in the holy place, you and your sons and your house with you. It has been given as an ordinance for you and an ordinance for your sons, of the sacrificial peace-offering of the children of Israel. They will bring the shoulder of the choice-offering, and the breast of the separation on the burnt offerings of the fat, to separate for a separation before Yahweh, and it will be a perpetual ordinance for you and your sons and your daughters with you, as Yahweh commanded Moses."

Moses diligently searched for the goat of the sin-offering, but it had been consumed by fire, and Moses was angry with Eleazar and Ithamar, the sons of Aaron, who were left, demanding, "Why did you not eat the sin-offering in the holy place? Because it is sacred that he has given you this to eat, that you might take away the sin of the congregation, and make atonement for them before Yahweh! The blood was not brought into the holy place! You will eat it inside, before Yahweh, as Yahweh commanded me!"

Aaron said to Moses, "If they have brought near today their sin-offerings, and their whole burnt offerings before Yahweh and these events have happened to me, and yet I should eat today of the sin-offering, would it be pleasing to Yahweh?"

Moses heard it, and it pleased him.

CHAPTER 11

Yahweh said to Moses and Aaron, "Tell the sons of Israel, 'These are the animals which you may eat out of all animals that are on the land. Every animal that has split hooves or divided claws, and chews the cud among animals, these you may eat. But these you may not eat, of those that chew the cud, and of those that have split hooves, and divide claws, the camel, because it chews the cud, but does not have split hooves, this is unclean to you. The rabbit, because it chews the cud, but does not have split hooves, is unclean to you. The hare, because it does not chew the cud, and does not have split hooves, is unclean to you. The hog, because this animal has split hooves and makes claws of the hoof, but it does not chew the cud, is unclean to you. You will not eat of their flesh, and you will not touch their carcasses; these are unclean to you.'"

"These are what you may eat of all that are in the waters: all things that have fins and scales in the waters, and the seas, and the brooks, these you may eat. All things which have no fins or scales in the water, or the seas, and the brooks, of all which the waters produce, and of every mind living in the water, are an abomination, and they will be abominations to you. You may not eat of their flesh, and you will detest their carcasses. All things that have no fins or scales of those that are in the waters, these are an abomination to you."

"These are the things which you will detest among birds, and they will not be eaten, they are an abomination: the eagle and the bearded vulture, and the sea-eagle. The vulture, and the falcon, and those like them, and the sparrow, and the owl, and the cormorant, and those like them, and every raven, and the birds like them, and the hawk and those like them, and the night-raven and the cormorant and the stork, and the red-bill, and the pelican, and swan, and the heron, and the lapwing, and those like them, and the hoopoe and the bat. All winged creatures that creep, which go on four feet, are abominations to you."

"But these you may eat of the creeping winged animals, which go on four feet, which have legs above their feet, to leap with on the land. These you may eat of them: the cater-pillar and those like it, and the attacus and those like it, and the cantharus and those like it, and the locust and those like it."

"Every creeping thing from among the birds, which has four feet, is an abomination to you. These will defile you. Everyone who touches their carcasses will be unclean until the evening. Everyone who touches their dead bodies will wash his garments and will be unclean until the evening."

"Whichever among the animals that has split hooves and makes claws, and does not chew the cud, will be unclean to you. Everyone who touches their dead bodies will be unclean until evening. All of the wild animals that move on four feet are unclean to you. Everyone who touches their dead bodies will be unclean until evening. He who takes their dead bodies will wash his clothes and will be unclean until evening. These are unclean to you. These are unclean to you: the reptiles on the land, the weasel, and the mouse, and the lizard, the ferret, and the chameleon, and the salamander, and the newt, and the mole. These are unclean to you: all the reptiles which are on the land. Everyone who touches their carcasses will be unclean until evening."

"On whatever one of their dead bodies will fall, it, will be unclean. Whatever wooden vessel, or garment, or skin, or sack it is, every vessel in which work should be done will be dipped in water, and will be unclean until evening, and then it will be clean. Every earthen vessel into which one of these things will fall, whatever is inside it, will be unclean, and it will be broken. All food that is eaten, on which water will come from such a vessel, will be unclean, and every beverage that is drunk in any such vessel will be unclean. Everything on which their dead bodies will be unclean; ovens and stands for jars will be broken down: these are unclean, and they will be unclean to you. Only if the water is from fountains of water or a pool, or a confluence of water, it will be clean, but he who touches their carcasses will be unclean."

"If one of their carcasses should fall on any grain seed which is to be sown, it will be clean. But if water is poured on any seed, and one of their dead bodies falls on it, it is unclean to you."

"If one of the livestock dies, which is lawful for you to eat, anyone who touches their carcasses will be unclean until evening. He that eats their carcasses will wash his garments, and be unclean until evening, and he that carries any of their carcasses will wash his garments, and bathe himself in water, and be unclean until evening."

"Every reptile that creeps on the land will be an abomination to you. It will not be eaten. Every animal that creeps on its belly, and everyone that goes on four feet continually, which abounds with feet among all the reptiles creeping on the land, you will not eat it, for it is an abomination to you. You will not defile your minds with any of the reptiles that creep on the land, and you will not be polluted with them, and you will not be unclean by them."

"For I am the lord of the gods, and you will be sanctified, and you will be holy, because I, Yahweh your God, am holy, and you will not defile your minds with any of the reptiles creeping on the land. For I am Yahweh, who brought you up out of the land of Egypt to be your god,[1] and you will be holy, for I Yahweh am holy. This is the law concerning animals and birds and every living creature moving in the water, and every living creature creeping on the land, to distinguish between the unclean and the clean, and between those that give birth alive, that should be eaten, and those that give birth alive, that should not be eaten."

CHAPTER 11 NOTES

1 Codex Vaticanus: umōn TS (ⲨⲘⲱⲚⲞ̄Ⲥ). Translation: your god

• LXX 29: umōn ΚS (υμων ΚϹ). Translation: your Lord

• LXX 72: umin teos (υμιν θϵοσ). Translation: y'all's god

CHAPTER 11

- Leningrad Codex: lākem lē'lōhîm (לָכֶם לֵאלֹהִים). Translation: for you the goddesses (in Hebrew, or "gods" in Aramaic, or "god" in Neo-Assyrian)

- Peshitta: ålhå (ܐܠܗܐ). Translation: god

- Targum Onkelos: elah (אֱלָה). Translation: god

- Targum Jerusalem: alaha (אֱלָהָא). Translation: God

- Sahidic manuscript 2006: touaab peje pjoeis (ϯⲟⲩⲁⲁⲃ ⲡⲉϫⲉ ⲡϫⲟⲉⲓⲥ). Translation: I am to be sanctified called the master

This paragraph has not survived intact in any of the fragments of Leviticus found among the Dead Sea Scrolls, however, the word ålhym is found in other fragments of Leviticus, confirming it was used in the same place that the Masoretic Text uses it.

- Dead Sea Scroll 1QpaleoLev: ålhym (ⵎⵣⴹⵍⴼ)

- Dead Sea Scroll 4QLev-Numᵃ: ålhym (𐤌𐤉𐤄𐤋𐤀)

- Dead Sea Scroll 4QLevᵇ: ålhym (אׁלׁהׁיׁמׁ)

- Dead Sea Scroll 11QpaleoLevᵃ: ålhym (ⵎⵣⴹⴼ)

The word in the Leningrad Codex is commonly translated as "God," but is a plural form of the Aramaic ålhå (𐡍𐡕𐡋𐡍), meaning "gods," or a plural form of the Hebrew 'ēlâ (אֱלָה) meaning "goddesses." The term ålhym (ⵝⵣⴹⵍⴼ), and ålhym (ⵏⵏⵍⵏ) are also direct transcriptions of the Assyrian cuneiform word elium (𒀭𒈨𒌍), which by the Iron Age meant "god," explaining why the Aramaic term ålhym (ⵏⵏⵍⵏ) would have been interpreted as "god" by the Greek translators.

63

CHAPTER 12

Yahweh said to Moses, "Tell the children of Israel, 'Whichever woman has conceived and born a male child will be unclean seven days, she will be unclean according to the days of separation for her monthly flow. On the eighth day, she will circumcise the flesh of his foreskin. For thirty-three days, she will continue in her unclean blood. She will touch nothing holy and will not enter the sanctuary until the days of her purification are fulfilled. But if she should have borne a female child, then she will be unclean twice seven days, according to the time of her monthly flow, and for sixty-six days will she remain in her unclean blood."

"When the days of her purification have been fulfilled for a son or a daughter, she will bring an undamaged lamb of a year old for a whole burnt offering, and a young pigeon or turtle-dove for a sin-offering to the door of the tabernacle of witness, to the priest. He will present it before Yahweh, and the priest will make atonement for her and will purge her from the fountain of her blood. This is the law of she who carries a male or a female. If she can't afford a lamb, then will she take two turtle-doves or two young pigeons, one for a whole burnt offering, and one for a sin-offering, and the priest will make atonement for her, and she will be purified.'"

CHAPTER 13

Yahweh said to Moses and Aaron, "If any man should have on the skin of his flesh a bright, clear spot, and there should be on the skin of his flesh a plague of leprosy, he will be brought to Aaron the priest, or one of his sons the priests. The priest will view the spot in the skin of his flesh, and if the hair in the spot is changed to white, and the appearance of the spot is below the skin of the flesh, it is a plague of leprosy, and the priest will look on it and pronounce him unclean. But if the spot is clear and white in the skin of his flesh, yet the appearance is not deep below the skin, and its hair has not changed to white hair, but it is dark, then the priest will separate him who has the spot for seven days, and the priest will look on the spot the seventh day."

"Look, if the spot remains as before, if the spot has not spread in the skin, then the priest will separate him the second time for seven days. The priest will look at him the second time on the seventh day. And, look, if the spot is dark and the spot has not spread in the skin, then the priest will pronounce him clean. For it is just a mark, and the man will wash his garments and be clean. But if the bright spot should have changed and spread in the skin after the priest has seen him to purify him, then he will appear the second time to the priest, and the priest will look at him. Look, if the mark has spread in the skin, then the priest will pronounce him unclean. It is leprosy."

CHAPTER 13

"If a man has a plague of leprosy, then he will come to the priest. The priest will look, and if it is a white spot in the skin, and it has changed the hair to white, and there is some of the sound part of the quick flesh in the sore, it is leprosy growing old in the skin of the flesh, and the priest will pronounce him unclean and will separate him because he is unclean. If leprosy should have come out very evidently in the skin, and leprosy should cover all the skin of the patient from the head to the feet, wherever the priest will look, then the priest will see, and, leprosy has covered all the skin of the flesh, and the priest will pronounce him clean of the plague because it has changed all to white, it is clean."

"But on any day the quick flesh appears on him, he will be pronounced unclean. The priest will look on the sound flesh, and the sound flesh will prove him to be unclean, for it is unclean, it is leprosy. But if the sound flesh is restored and changed to white, then he will come to the priest, and the priest will see him, and if the plague is turned white, then the priest will pronounce the patient clean. He is clean. If the flesh should have become an ulcer in his skin and should be healed, and there should be in the place of the ulcer a white sore, or one looking white and bright, or fiery, and it will be seen by the priest; then the priest will look, and if the appearance is beneath the skin, and its hair has changed to white, then the priest will pronounce him unclean because it is leprosy, it has broken out in the ulcer."

"But if the priest looks, and there is no white hair on it, and it is not below the skin of the flesh, and it is dark-colored; then the priest will separate him seven days. But if it manifests itself over the skin, then the priest will pronounce him unclean: it is a plague of leprosy. It has broken out in an ulcer. But if the bright spot should remain in its place and not spread, it is the scar of the ulcer, and the priest will pronounce him clean. If the flesh of his skin in a state of fiery inflammation, and there is in his skin the part which is healed from the inflammation, bright, clear, and white, mixed with red or very white, then the priest will look at him, and, if the white hair is changed to a bright color, and its appearance is lower than the skin, it is leprosy, it has broken out in the inflammation, and the priest will pronounce him unclean. It is a plague of leprosy."

"But if the priest should look, and there is no white hair in the bright spot, and it is not lower than the skin, and it is dark, then the priest will separate him seven days. The priest will look at him on the seventh day, and if the spot has spread in the skin, then the priest will pronounce him unclean. It is a plague of leprosy. It has broken out in an ulcer. But if the bright spot remains stationary, and has not spread in the skin, but the sore should be dark, it is a scar of inflammation, and the priest will pronounce him clean, for it is the mark of the inflammation."

"If a man or a woman has in them a plague of leprosy in the head or the beard, then the priest will look on the plague, and, if the appearance is beneath the skin, and in it, there is thin yellowish hair, then the priest will pronounce him unclean. It is dandruff, it is the leprosy of the head or leprosy of the beard. If the priest sees the plague of dandruff, and the appearance is not beneath the skin, and there is no yellowish hair in it, then the priest will set apart him who has the plague of dandruff seven days. The priest will look at the plague on the seventh day, and if the dandruff is not spread, and there is no yellowish hair on it, and the appearance of dandruff is not hollow under the skin, then the skin will be shaven, but the dandruff will not be shaven, and the priest will set aside the person having the dandruff the second time for seven days. The priest will see the dandruff on the seventh day, and see if the dandruff has not spread in the skin after the man's being shaved, and the appearance of the dandruff is not hollow beneath the skin, then the priest will pronounce him clean, and he will wash his garments, and be clean. But if the dandruff is indeed spread in the skin after he has been purified, then the priest will look, and, if the dandruff is spread in the skin, the priest will not examine concerning the yellow hair, for he is unclean. But if the dandruff remains before him in its place, and a dark hair should have risen in it, the scurf is healed. He is clean, and the priest will pronounce him clean."

"If a man or woman should have on the skin of their flesh bright whiteness spots, then the priest will look, and if there are bright spots of a bright whiteness in the skin of their flesh, it is eczema. It burst out in the skin of his flesh. He is clean."

"If anyone's head should lose the hair, he is only bald; he is clean. If his head should lose the hair in front, he is bald. He is clean. If there should be in his baldness of head, or his baldness of forehead, a white or fiery plague, it is leprosy in his baldness of head or baldness of forehead. The priest will look on him, and if the appearance of the plague is white or inflamed in his baldness of head or baldness in front, as the appearance of leprosy in the skin of his flesh, he is a leprous man: the priest will surely pronounce him unclean, his plague is in his head. The leper in whom the plague is, let his garments be loosened, and his head uncovered, and let him have a covering put on his mouth, and he will be called unclean. In the days in which the plague is on him, being unclean, he will be considered unclean. He will dwell apart; his place of residence will be outside the camp."

"If a garment has in it the plague of leprosy, a garment of wool, or a garment of flax, either in the warp or in the woof, or the linen, or in the woolen threads, or skin, or in any workmanship of skin, and the plague is greenish or reddish in the skin, or in the garment, either in the warp, or in the woof, or in any utensil of skin, it is a plague of leprosy, and he will show it to the priest. The priest will look on the plague, and the priest will set apart that which has the plague seven days. The priest will look at the plague on the seventh day, and if the plague is spread in the garment, either in the warp or in the woof, or the skin, in whatever things may be used in their workmanship, the plague is confirmed leprosy. It is unclean. He will burn the garment, either the warp or woof in woolen garments or in flaxen or in any utensil of skin, in which there may be the plague; because it is confirmed leprosy; it will be burnt with fire."

CHAPTER 13

"If the priest should see, and the plague has not spread in the garments, either in the warp or in the woof, or any utensil of skin, then the priest will give directions, and one will wash that on which there may have been the plague, and the priest will set it aside a second time for seven days. The priest will look on it after the plague has been washed, and if this, even the plague, has not changed its appearance, and the plague does not spread, it is unclean. It will be burnt with fire. It is fixed in the garment, in the warp, or in the woof."

"If the priest should look, and the spot is dark after it has been washed, he will tear it off from the garment, either from the warp or from the woof, or the skin. If it should still appear in the garment, either in the warp or in the woof, or in any article of skin, it is leprosy bursting out. That which has the plague in it will be burnt with fire. The garment, or the warp, or the woof, or any article of skin, which will be washed, and the plague depart from it, will also be washed again, and will be clean. This is the law of the plague of leprosy of a woolen or linen garment, either of the warp, or woof, or any leather article, to pronounce it clean or unclean."

CHAPTER 14

Yahweh said to Moses, "This is the law of the leper. On whatever day he has been cleansed, then will he be brought to the priest. The priest will come out of the camp, and the priest will look, and the plague of leprosy will be removed from the leper. The priest will give directions, and they will take for him that is cleansed two clean live birds, and cedarwood, and spun scarlet, and hyssop. The priest will give direction, and they will kill one bird over an earthen vessel over running water. As for the living bird, he will take it, and the cedarwood, and the spun scarlet, and the hyssop, and he will dip them and the living bird into the blood of the bird that was slain over running water. He will sprinkle seven times on him that was cleansed of his leprosy, and he will be clean, and he will let go the living bird into the field."

"The man that has been cleansed will wash his garments, and will shave off all his hair, and will wash in water, and will be clean, and after that, he will go into the camp and will remain out of his house seven days. It will come to pass on the seventh day, he will shave off all his hair on his head, and his beard, and his eyebrows, even all his hair will he shave, and he will wash his garments, and wash his body with water, and will be clean. On the eighth day, he will take two undamaged one-year-old lambs, and an undamaged one-year-old ewe lamb, and three-tenths of fine flour for sacrifice kneaded with oil, and one small cup of oil. The priest who

CHAPTER 14

cleanses will present the man under purification, and these offerings before Yahweh, at the door of the tabernacle of witness. The priest will take one lamb, and offer him for a trespass-offering, and the cup of oil, and set them apart for a special offering before Yahweh."

"They will kill the lamb in the place where they kill the whole burnt offerings, and the sin-offerings, in the holy places, as if it were a sin-offering or trespass-offering. It belongs to the priest; it is holiest. The priest will take the blood of the trespass-offering, and the priest will put it on the tip of the right ear of the person under cleansing, and the thumb of his right hand, and the big toe of his right foot. The priest will take the cup of oil and will pour it on his own left hand. He will dip the finger of his right hand into some of the oil that is in his left hand, and he will sprinkle with his finger seven times before Yahweh."

"The remaining oil that is in his hand, the priest will put on the tip of the right ear of him that is under cleansing, and on the thumb of his right hand, and the big toe of his right foot, in place of the blood of the trespass-offering. The remaining oil that is in the hand of the priest, the priest will put on the head of the cleansed leper, and the priest will make atonement for him before Yahweh. The priest will sacrifice the sin-offering, and the priest will make atonement for the person under purification to cleanse him from his sin, and afterward, the priest will kill the whole burnt offering. The priest will offer the whole burnt offering, and the

74

sacrifice on the altar before Yahweh, and the priest will make atonement for him, and he will be cleansed."

"If he is poor, and can't afford much, he can take one lamb for his transgression for a separate-offering, to make appeasement for him, and a tenth measure of fine flour mingled with oil for a sacrifice, and one cup of oil, and two turtledoves, or two young pigeons, as he can afford, and the one will be for a sin-offering, and the other for a whole burnt offering. He will bring them on the eighth day, to purify him, to the priest, to the door of the tabernacle of witness before Yahweh. The priest will take the lamb of the trespass-offering, and the cup of oil, and place them for a set-offering before Yahweh. He will kill the lamb of the trespass-offering, and the priest will take of the blood of the trespass-offering, and put it on the tip of the right ear of him that is under purification, and the thumb of his right hand, and on the big toe of his right foot."

"The priest will pour the oil on his own left hand. The priest will sprinkle with the finger of his right hand some of the oil that is in his left hand seven times before Yahweh. The priest will put of the oil that is on his hand on the tip of the right ear of him that is under purification, and on the thumb of his right hand, and the big toe of his right foot, on the place of the blood of the trespass-offering. That which is left of the oil which is in the hand of the priest he will put on the head of him that is purged, and the priest will make atonement for him before Yahweh. He will offer one of the turtledoves or the young pigeons, as he can afford it, the one for a sin-offering, the other for a whole burnt offering with the meat-offering, and the priest will make atonement before Yahweh for him that is under purification. This is the law for him in whom is the plague of leprosy, and who can't afford the offerings for his purification."

Yahweh said to Moses and Aaron, "When you enter into the land of the Canaanites, which I give you for a possession, and I will put the plague of leprosy in the houses of the land of your possession, then the owner of the house will come and report to the priest, saying, 'I have seen as it were a plague in the house.' The priest will give orders to remove the furniture from the house before the priest comes in to see the plague, and so none of the things in the house will become unclean, and afterward, the priest will go in to examine the house. He will look at the plague, and if the plague is in the walls of the house, he will see greenish or reddish cavities, and the appearance of them will be beneath the surface of the walls."

"The priest will exit the house by the door, and the priest will quarantine the house for seven days. The priest will return on the seventh day and view the house, and, if the plague is spread in the walls of the house, then the priest will give orders, and they will take away the stones in which the plague is, and will cast them out of the city into an unclean place. They will scrape the inside of the house and will pour out the dust scraped off outside the city into an unclean place. They will take other scraped stones, and put them in the place of the former stones, and they will take other plaster and plaster the house."

"If the plague should return, and break out in the house after they have taken away the stones and after the house is scraped, and after it has been plastered, then the priest will go in and see if the plague is spread in the house; it is confirmed leprosy in the house. It is unclean. They will take down the house, and its timbers and its stones, and they will carry out all the mortar outside of the city into an unclean place. He that goes into the house at any time, during its separation, will be unclean until evening. He that sleeps in the house will wash his garments, and be unclean until evening, and he that eats in the house will wash his garments, and be unclean until evening."

"If the priest arrives and enters and sees the plague has not at all spread in the house after the house has been plastered, then the priest will declare the house clean because the plague is healed. He will take two clean living birds, and cedarwood, and spun scarlet, and hyssop. He will kill one bird in an earthen vessel over running water. He will take the cedarwood, the spun scarlet, and the hyssop, and the living bird, and will dip it into the blood of the bird slain over running water, and with them, he will sprinkle the house seven times. He will purify the house with the blood of the bird, and with the running water, and with the living bird, and with the cedarwood, and with the hyssop, and with the spun scarlet. He will let the living bird go out of the city into the field, and will make atonement for the house, and it will be clean. This is the law concerning every plague of leprosy and dandruff, and leprosy of a garment, and a house, and a sore, and a clear spot, and a shining one, and of declaring in what day it is unclean, and in what day it will be purged."

This is the law of leprosy.

CHAPTER 15

Yahweh said to Moses and Aaron, "Speak to the children of Israel, and you will say to them, 'Any man that has an issue out of his body, his issue is unclean. This is the law of his uncleanness. Whoever has gonorrhea coming out of his body, this is his uncleanness in him by reason of the issue, by which his body is affected through the issue: all the days of the issue of his body, by which his body is affected through the issue, there is his uncleanness. Every bed on which he who has the issue will lie is unclean, and every seat on which he that has the issue may happen to sit, will be unclean. The man who touches his bed will wash his garments and bathe himself in water and will be unclean until evening."

"Whoever sits on the seat on which he who has the issue may have sat, will wash his garments, and bathe himself in water, and will be unclean until evening. He that touches the skin of him that has the issue, will wash his garments and bathe himself in water, and will be unclean until evening. If he who has the issue should spit on one who is clean, that person will wash his garments, bathe himself in water, and be unclean until evening. Every donkey's saddle, on which the man with the issue has mounted, will be unclean until evening. Everyone who touches whatever has been under him will be unclean until evening, and he that takes them up will wash his garments, and bathe himself in water, and will be unclean until evening."

"Whoever he is that has the issue will touch, if he has not rinsed his hands in water, he will wash his garments, and bathe his body in water, and will be unclean until evening. The earthen vessel that has the issue will happen to touch will be broken, and a wooden vessel will be washed with water and will be clean. And if he who has the issue should be cleansed of his issue, then he will count for himself seven days for his purification, and he will wash his garments and bathe his body in water and will be clean. On the eighth day, he will take to himself two turtledoves or two young pigeons, and he will bring them before Yahweh to the doors of the tabernacle of witness and will give them to the priest. The priest will offer them one for a sin-offering, and the other for a whole burnt offering, and the priest will make atonement for him before Yahweh for his issue."

"The man whose seed of copulation will happen to come out from him will then wash his whole body and will be unclean until evening. Every garment and every skin on which there will be the seed of copulation will both be washed with water, and be unclean until evening. A woman, if a man lies with her and copulates with semen, they will both bathe themselves in water and will be unclean until evening. The woman who has an issue of blood, when her issue is in her body, will be separated for seven days. Everyone who touches her will be unclean until evening. Everything on which she will lie in her separation will be unclean, and whatever she will sit on will be unclean. Whoever touches her bed will wash his garments, and bathe his body in water, and will be unclean until evening. And everyone who touches any vessel on which she will sit, will wash his garments and bathe himself in water, and will be unclean until evening. Whether it is while she is on her bed, or on a seat which she may happen to sit on when he touches her, he will be unclean until evening. If anyone will lie with her, and her uncleanness is on him, he will be unclean seven days, and every bed on which he has lain will be unclean."

"If a woman has an issue of blood many days, not in the time of her separation, if the blood should also flow after her separation, all the days of the issue of her uncleanness will be as the days of her separation. She will be unclean. Every bed on which she will lie all the days of her flow will be to her as the bed of her separation, and every seat on which she will sit will be unclean according to the uncleanness of her separation. Everyone who touches it will be unclean, and he will wash his garments, bathe his body in water, and will be unclean until evening. But if she is cleansed from her flow, then she will count for herself seven days, and afterward, she will be considered clean. On the eighth day, she will take two turtle-doves, or two young pigeons, and will bring them to the priest, to the door of the tabernacle of witness. The priest will offer one for a sin-offering, and the other for a whole burnt offering, and the priest will make atonement for her before Yahweh for her unclean flow."

"You will make the children of Israel to beware of their uncleannesses, so they will not die for their uncleanness, in polluting my tabernacle that is among them."

CHAPTER 15

This is the law of the man who has an issue, and if one discharges seed of copulation, so that he should be polluted by it. This is the law for her that has the issue of blood in her separation, and as to the person who has an issue of seed, in his issue: it is a law for the male and the female, and for the man who has lain with her that is set apart.

CHAPTER 16

Yahweh spoke to Moses after the two sons of Aaron died when bringing strange fire before Yahweh. Yahweh said to Moses, "Speak to Aaron your brother, and let him not come in at all times into the holy place within the veil before the lid, which is on the ark of the testimony, and he will not die, for I will appear in a cloud on the lid. Aaron entered into the holy place: with a calf of the herd for a sin-offering, and having a ram for a whole burnt offering. He will put on the consecrated linen tunic, and he has on his flesh the linen trousers, and will gird himself with a linen girdle, and will put on the linen cap; they are holy garments, and he will bathe all his body in water, and will put them on."

"He will take from the congregation of the children of Israel two kids of the goats for a sin-offering, and one lamb for a whole burnt offering. Aaron will bring the calf for his own sin-offering and will make atonement for himself and his house. He will take the two goats, and place them before Yahweh by the door of the tabernacle of witness. Aaron will cast lots on the two goats, one lot for Yahweh, and the other for the scapegoat.[1] Aaron will bring forward the goat on which the lot for Yahweh fell, and will offer him for a sin-offering. The goat on which the lot of the scapegoat came, he will present alive before Yahweh, to make atonement on him, to send him away as a scapegoat, and he will send him into the wilderness."

CHAPTER 16

"Aaron will bring the calf for his sin, and he will make atonement for himself and for his house, and he will kill the calf for his sin-offering. He will take his censer full of coals of fire off the altar, which is before Yahweh, and he will fill his hands with fine compound incense and will bring it within the veil. He will put the incense on the fire before Yahweh, and the smoke of the incense will cover the mercy-seat over the tables of testimony, and he will not die. He will take of the blood of the calf, and sprinkle with his finger on the mercy-seat towards the east: before the mercy-seat will he sprinkle seven times of the blood with his finger. He will kill the goat for the sin-offering that is for the people before Yahweh, and he will bring in its blood within the veil, and will do with its blood as he did with the blood of the calf, and will sprinkle its blood on the mercy-seat, in front of the mercy-seat. He will make atonement for the sanctuary on account of the uncleanness of the children of Israel, and their trespasses in the matter of all their sins, and thus will he do to the tabernacle of witness established among them in the middle of their uncleanness."

"There will be no man in the tabernacle of witness when he goes in to make atonement in the holy place, until he has come out. He will make atonement for himself, and his house, and all the congregation of the children of Israel. He will come out to the altar that is before Yahweh, and he will make atonement on it, and he will take the blood of the calf, and the blood of the goat, and will put it on the horns of the altar and around it. He will sprinkle some of the blood on it seven times with his finger and will purge it, and hallow it from the uncleanness of the children of Israel. He will finish making atonement for the sanctuary and for the tabernacle of witness, and the altar, and he will make a cleansing for the priests, and he will bring the living goat. Aaron will lay his hands on the head of the live goat, and he will declare over him all the iniquities of the children of Israel, and all their unrighteousness, and all their sins, and he will lay them on the head of the live goat and will send him by the hand of a ready man into the wilderness. The goat will bear their unrighteousness on him into a desert land, and Aaron will send away the goat into the wilderness."

"Aaron will enter into the tabernacle of witness and will take off the linen garment, which he had put on, as he entered into the holy place, and will lay it down. He will bathe his body in water in the holy place, and will put on his clothing, and will go out and offer the whole burnt offering for himself and the whole burnt offering for the people: and will make atonement for himself and for his house, and for the people, as for the priests. He will offer the fat for the sin-offering on the altar. He that sends forth the goat that has been set apart to be let go, will wash his garments, and bathe his body in water, and afterward will enter into the camp. The calf for the sin-offering, and the goat for the sin-offering, whose blood was brought in to make atonement in the holy place, they will carry out of the camp, and burn them with fire, even their skins and their flesh and their dung. He that burns them will wash his garments, and bathe his body in water, and afterward, he will enter into the camp. This will be a perpetual statute for you, in the seventh month, on the tenth day of the month, you will humble your minds, and will do no work, nor the native and the stranger who lives among you. For on this day he will make an atonement for you, to cleanse you from all your sins before Yahweh, and you will be purged. This will be for you the holiest sabbath, a rest, and you will humble your minds; it is a perpetual ordinance. The priest, whoever they will anoint, will make atonement, and whoever they will consecrate to exercise the priestly office after his father, and he will put on the linen robe, the holy garment. He will make atonement for the holiest place, and the tabernacle of witness, and he will make atonement for the altar, and for the priests, and he will make atonement for all the congregation. This will be to you a perpetual statute to make atonement for the children of Israel for all their sins."

It will be done once a year, as Yahweh commanded Moses.

CHAPTER 16 NOTES

1 Codex Vaticanus: ḥimarous (ⲭⲓⲘⲀⲢⲞⲨⲤ). Translation: male-goat-kid

- LXX 55: trágos (ⲦⲢⲀⲅⲅⲞⲤ). Translation: billy-goat
- Leningrad Codex: śə'îrê (שָׂעִירֵי). Translation: hairy
- DSS 4QLev-Numᵃ: šŏyry (שׁעירי)
- Peshitta: ŏzå (ܥܙܐ). Translation: she-goat
- Targum Onkelos: səpîrê (צְפִירֵי). Translation: he-goats
- Targum Jerusalem: səpîrê (צְפִירֵי). Translation: he-goats

• Sahidic manuscript 2006: nbaampe (ⲛⲃⲁⲁⲙⲡⲉ). Translation: hairy goats

The Hebrew word is generally believed to be a variation of the Greek word satyr (σάτυρος), itself possibly based on an older Canaanite term, however, the Greeks did not use the word satyr, instead, translating the word as male-goat-kid (χιμάρους), indicating that they did not consider the sacrifice to be a satyr. Both the Peshitta and Targum Onkelos use the Aramaic word for 'she-goat(s).'

CHAPTER 17

Yahweh said to Moses, "Speak to Aaron and to his sons, and to all the children of Israel, and say to them, 'This is the word which Yahweh has commanded, "Every man of the children of Israel, or of the strangers dwelling among you, who will kill a calf, or a sheep, or a goat in the camp, or who will kill it out of the camp, and will not bring it to the door of the tabernacle of witness." To sacrifice it for a whole burnt offering or peace-offering to Yahweh, to be acceptable for a sweet-smelling savor, whoever kills it outside, and will not bring it to the door of the tabernacle of witness, to offer it as a gift to Yahweh before the tabernacle of Yahweh. Blood will be imputed to that man, as he has shed blood. That mind will be cut off from his people.'"

"'The children of Israel may offer their sacrifices, all that they will kill in the fields, and bring them to Yahweh to the doors of the tabernacle of witness to the priest, and they will sacrifice them as a peace-offering to Yahweh. The priest will pour the blood on the altar round about before Yahweh by the doors of the tabernacle of witness and will offer the fat for a sweet-smelling savor to Yahweh. They will no longer offer their sacrifices to vain gods after which they go a whoring, it will be a perpetual statute to you for your generations.'"

"You will say to them, 'Whatever man of the children of Israel, or the sons of the proselytes dwelling among you, will offer a whole burnt offering or a sacrifice, and will not bring it to the door of the tabernacle of witness to sacrifice it to Yahweh, that man will be destroyed from among his people. Whatever man of the children of Israel, or the strangers dwelling among you, will eat any blood, I will even set my face against that mind that eats blood, and will destroy it from its people. For the life of the flesh is its blood, and I have given it to you on the altar to make atonement for your minds; for its blood will make atonement for the mind.'"

"'Therefore I said to the children of Israel, 'No mind of you will eat blood, and the stranger that lives among you will not eat blood.' Whatever man of the children of Israel, or the strangers dwelling among you will take any animal in hunting, animal, or bird, which is eaten, then he will pour out the blood, and cover it in the dust. For the blood of all flesh is its life, and I said to the children of Israel, 'You will not eat the blood of any flesh,' for the life of all flesh is its blood. Everyone who eats it will be destroyed. Every mind which eats that which has died itself, or is taken of animals, either among the natives or among the strangers, will wash his garments, and bathe himself in water, and will be unclean until evening: then will he be clean. But if he does not wash his garments, and does not bathe his body in water, then will he bear his iniquity.'"

CHAPTER 18

Yahweh commanded Moses, "Speak to the children of Israel and say to them, 'I am the lord of the gods. You will not do according to the ways of Egypt, in which you lived, and according to the ways of the land of Canaan, into which I bring you. You will not do, and you will not follow their ordinances. You will observe my judgments, and will keep my ordinances, and will follow them. I am the lord of the gods! So you will keep all my ordinances, and all my judgments, and do them, which if a man does, he will live in them! I am the lord of the gods!'"

"No man will draw near to any of his near family members and uncover their nakedness! I am Yahweh! You will not uncover the nakedness of your father, or the nakedness of your mother, for she is your mother! You will not uncover her nakedness. You will not uncover the nakedness of your father's wife; it is your father's nakedness. You will not uncover the nakedness of your sister or your father or your mother, born at home or abroad. The nakedness of your granddaughter you will not uncover because it is your nakedness. You will not uncover the nakedness of the daughter of your father's wife; she is your sister by the same father, you will not uncover her nakedness. You will not uncover the nakedness of your father's sister. She is near the family of your father. You will not uncover the nakedness of your mother's sister. She is near the family of your mother.

CHAPTER 18

You will not uncover the nakedness of your father's brother, and you will not go into his wife. She is your relation. You will not uncover the nakedness of your daughter-in-law, for she is your son's wife; you will not uncover her nakedness. You will not uncover the nakedness of your brother's wife. It is your brother's nakedness. The nakedness of a woman and her daughter will you not uncover, nor will you take her granddaughter to uncover their nakedness. They are your family, and it is inappropriate."

"You will not take your wife's sister in addition to her while she is still alive, as a rival, to uncover their nakedness together. You will not go into a woman during her separation for her uncleanness, to uncover her nakedness. You will not lie with your neighbor's wife, to defile yourself with her. You will not give of your seed to serve Moloch,[1] and you will not profane my holy name. I am Yahweh."

"You will not lie with a male as with a woman, for it is an abomination. Neither will you lie with any quadruped for copulation, to be polluted with it. Neither will a woman present herself before any quadruped to have intercourse with it, for it is an abomination."

CHAPTER 18 NOTES

1 Codex Vaticanus: arḫonti (ΑϷΧΟΝΤΙ). Translation: ruler
- Leningrad Codex: Mōlek (מֹלֶךְ). Translation: Moloch

- Peshitta: lmbtnw nwkrytå (ܠܡܒܛܢܘ ܢܘܟܪܝܬܐ). Translation: the womb of (feminine) foreigners
  - Targum Onkelos: Môlek (מוֹלֶךְ). Translation: Moloch
  - Targum Jerusalem: bat ammin (בַּת עַמְמִין). Translation: daughter of the (foreign) peoples
    - Sahidic manuscript 2006: arǩōn (ⲁⲣⲭⲱⲛ). Translation: ruler

The meaning of this verse has been debated for thousands of years. The Greek translation treated the word as a human "ruler," suggesting a prohibition on sending one's children to fight for a ruler, presumably other than the king of Jerusalem. The Hebrew translation, and the Aramaic Targum Onkelos both use the name Molech.

As Leviticus was almost certainly written in Judahite, the precursor to Classical Hebrew, the original word would have been mlk (𐤌𐤋𐤊), meaning 'king.' All records related to the translation indicate the Greek translation was made from an Aramaic translation, meaning the would would have been mlkå (𐡌𐡋𐡊𐡀), which means 'king' or 'ruler.' The significant deviation found in the Peshitta and Targum Jerusalem appears to be a substitution made after Molech worship had disappeared, and when the Judahite leaders were trying to suppress intermarriage with other nations. It may be a relic of Ezra's Aramaic Torah. As the name Molech is likely the original term used in the verse, the common English translation of Moloch is used in.

CHAPTER 19

Yahweh said Moses, Speak to the congregation of the children of Israel, and you will say to them, 'You will be holy, for I, Yahweh your God, am holy. Let every one of you respect his father and his mother, and you will keep my sabbaths. I am the lord of the gods!'"

"'You will not worship idols, and you will not make molten gods for yourselves. I am the lord of the gods!'"

"'If you sacrifice a peace-offering to Yahweh, you will offer it acceptable from yourselves. On whatever day you sacrifice it, it will be eaten, and on the following day, and if any is left until the third day, it will be thoroughly burnt with fire. If it should be at all eaten on the third day, it is unfit for sacrifice. It will not be accepted. He that eats it will bear his iniquity because he has profaned the holy things of Yahweh, and the minds that eat it will be destroyed from among their people. When you reap the harvest of your land, you will not complete the reaping of your field with exactness, and you will not gather that which falls from your reaping. You will not go over the gathering of your vineyard, nor will you gather the remaining grapes of your vineyard. You will leave them for the poor and the stranger. I am the lord of the gods!'"

"'You will not steal. You will not lie. You will not provide false witness as an informer against your neighbor. You will not swear unjustly by my name, and you will not profane the holy name of your god. I am the lord of the gods!"

"'You will not injure your neighbor, nor will you rob him, nor will the wages of your employee remain with you overnight. You will not revile the deaf, nor will you put a stumbling block in the way of the blind, and you will fear the lord of the gods. I am the lord of the gods! You will not act unjustly in judgment. You will not accept the existence of poor people, nor admire mighty people. You will judge your neighbor justly. You will not walk deceitfully among your people. You will not rise against the blood of your neighbor. I am the lord of the gods!'"

"'You will not hate your brother in your heart. You will not in any way rebuke your neighbor, so you will not bear sin on his account. Your hand will not avenge you, and you will not be angry with the children of your people. You will love your neighbor as yourself. I am Yahweh!'"

"'You will observe my law. You will not let your livestock mate with one of a different kind, and you will not sow your vineyard with diverse seed, and you will not put on yourself a mingled garment woven of two materials. If anyone lay carnally with a woman, and she should be a home-servant kept for a man, and she has not been ransomed, and her freedom has not been given to her, they will be visited with punishment; but they will not die, because she was not set at liberty. He will bring for his trespass to Yahweh to the door of the tabernacle of witness, a ram for a trespass-offering. The priest will make atonement for him with the ram of the trespass-offering, before Yahweh, for the sin which he sinned, and the sin which he sinned will be forgiven him.'"

"'When you enter into the land which Yahweh your God gives you, and will plant any fruit tree, then you will purge away its uncleanness. Its fruit will be unclean for you for three years, and will not be eaten. In the fourth year, all its fruit will be holy, a subject of praise to Yahweh. In the fifth year, you will eat the fruit; its produce is an increase for you. I am the lord of the gods!'"

"'Do not eat on the mountains, nor employ omens, nor divine by inspection of birds. You will not cut the hair of your head round, nor disfigure your beard. You will not make cuts in your body for a dead body, and you will not tattoo on yourselves any marks. I am the lord of the gods!'"

"'You will not profane your daughter and prostitute her, so the land will not go whoring, and the land will become filled with iniquity. You will keep my sabbaths, and revere my sanctuaries: I am Yahweh!'"

"'Do not follow your feelings, or you will pollute yourselves with them. I am the lord of the gods.'"

"'You will rise up before the gray head, and honor the face of the old man, and will fear your God, I am Yahweh your god.'"[1]

"'If a stranger should come to your land, you will not attack him. The stranger that comes to you will be among you as the native, and you will love him as yourself; for you were strangers in the land of Egypt: I am the lord of the gods!'"

CHAPTER 19

"'You will not act dishonestly in judgment, in measures and weights and scales. There will be among you just balances and just weights and just liquid measure. I am Yahweh, your God, who brought you out of the land of Egypt. You will keep all my laws and all my ordinances, and you will do them. I am Yahweh, your God!'"

CHAPTER 19 NOTES

1 Codex Vaticanus: kai fobēthēsē KN ton ṬN sou. Egō eimi KS o ṬS umōn (ΚΑΙ ΦΟΒΗΘΗCΗ Κ͞Ν ΤΟΝ Θ͞Ν COY ΕΓꙶ ΕΙΜΙ Κ͞C Ο Θ͞C Υ͞ΜꙶΝ) Translation: and fear lord the god of you. I am lord the god of you

- Leningrad Codex: wəyārē'tā mē'ĕlōhêkā 'ănî Yəhwâ (וְיָרֵאתָ מֵאֱלֹהֶיךָ אֲנִי יְהוָה). Translation: and fear god of yours I'm Yahweh

- Peshitta: ålå dḥl mn ålhå: ånå ånå mryå (ܐܠܐ ܕܚܠ ܡܢ ܐܠܗܐ: ܐܢܐ ܐܢܐ ܡܪܝܐ). Translation: unless being afraid of god: I am master

- Targum Onkelos: wətidhal mē'ĕlāhāk 'ānā' Yəyā (וְתִדְחַל מֵאֱלָהָךְ אֲנָא יְיָ). Translation: and be afraid of god of yours I'm Yahweh

- Targum Jerusalem: wətidhal mē'ĕlāhāk ănā' Yəyā (וְתִדְחַל מֵאֱלָהָךְ אֲנָא יְיָ). Translation: and be afraid of god of yours I'm Yahweh

- Sahidic manuscript 2006: ekerhote hētf mpjoeis peknoute. Anok gar pe pjoeis peknoute (ⲉⲕⲉⲣϩⲟⲧⲉ ϩⲏⲧϥ ⲙⲡϫⲟⲉⲓⲥ ⲡⲉⲕⲛⲟⲩⲧⲉ. ⲀⲚⲞⲔ ⲄⲀⲢ ⲡⲉ ⲡϫⲟⲉⲓⲥ ⲡⲉⲕⲛⲟⲩⲧⲉ). Translation: you must show reverence before the master your god. I indeed am the master your god.

- Sahidic manuscript 2044: ekerhote hētf mpeknoute. Anok gar pe pjoeis peknoute. (ⲉⲕⲉⲣϩⲟⲧⲉ ϩⲏⲧϥ ⲙⲡⲉⲕⲛⲟⲩⲧⲉ. ⲀⲚⲞⲔ ⲄⲀⲢ ⲡⲉ ⲡϫⲟⲉⲓⲥ ⲡⲉⲕⲛⲟⲩⲧⲉ). Translation: you must show reverence before your god. I indeed am the master your god.

CHAPTER 20

Yahweh said to Moses, "You will also tell the children of Israel, 'If there are any of the children of Israel, or of those who have become proselytes in Israel, who give their seed to Moloch,[1] let him be put to death. The nation on the land will stone him with stones. I will set my face against that man and will cut him off from his people, because he has given of his seed to Moloch, to defile my sanctuary, and profane the name of them that are consecrated to me. If the natives of the land should in any way overlook that man in giving of his seed to Moloch, so as not put him to death, then I will set my face against that man and his family, and I will destroy him, and all who have been of one mind with him, so that he should go a whoring to Moloch, from their people. The mind that will follow those who have in them divining spirits, or enchanters, to go a whoring after them; I will set my face against that mind and will destroy it from among its people. You will be holy, for I, Yahweh your God, am holy.'"

"'You will observe my ordinances, and do them. I am Yahweh, who sanctifies you. Every man who will speak evil of his father or his mother, let him die the death. Has he spoken evil of his father or his mother? He will be guilty."

"Whatever man will commit adultery with the wife of a man, or whoever will commit adultery with the wife of his neighbor, let them die the death, the adulterer and the adulteress."

Chapter 20

"If anyone should lie with his father's wife, he has uncovered his father's nakedness: let them both die the death, they are guilty. If anyone should lie with his daughter-in-law, let them both be put to death, for they have worked impiety, they are guilty."

"Whoever will lie with a male as with a woman, they have both worked abomination; let them die the death, they are guilty."

"Whoever will take a woman and her mother, it is iniquity: they will burn him and them with fire. So there will not be iniquity among you.'"

"Whoever lies with an animal, let him die the death, and you will kill the animal. Whatever woman approaches any animal to have intercourse with it, you will kill the woman and the animal. Let them die the death, they are guilty."

"Whoever will take his sister by his father or by his mother, and will see her nakedness, and she sees his nakedness, it is a reproach: they will be destroyed before the children of their family. He has uncovered his sister's nakedness; they will bear their sin."

"Whatever man will lie with a woman that is set apart for a flow, and will uncover her nakedness, he has uncovered her fountain, and she has uncovered the flow of her blood. They will both be destroyed from among their generation."

"You will not uncover the nakedness of your father's sister, or the sister of your mother. For that man has uncovered the nakedness of one near family: they will bear their iniquity."

CHAPTER 20

"Whoever lies with his near relative has uncovered the nakedness of one closely related to him. They will die childless."

"Whoever will take his brother's wife, it is uncleanness, he has uncovered his brother's nakedness, they will die childless."

"Keep all my ordinances, and my judgments, and you will do them, and the land will not be injured by you, which I bring you to live in. Don't follow in the customs of the nations which I drive out from before you; for they have done all these things, and I have abhorred them: and I said to you, You will inherit their land, and I will give it to you for a possession, a land flowing with milk and honey. I am Yahweh, your God, who has separated you from all people. You will make a distinction between the clean and the unclean livestock, and between clean and unclean birds, and you will not defile your minds with livestock, or with birds, or with any creeping things of the land, which I have separated for you because of uncleanness. You will be holy to me, because I, Yahweh your God, am holy, who separated you from all nations, to be mine."

"As for a man or woman, whoever of them has in them a divining spirit, or be an enchanter, let them both die the death. You will stone them with stones, they are guilty."

CHAPTER 20 NOTES

1 Codex Vaticanus: arḫonti (ΛϷΧΟΝΤΙ). Translation: ruler

- LXX 75: tō arḫonti (τοο αρχ⊕ḭι). Translation: the ruler

- LXX 106: Molekh (Μολϭχ). Translation: Moloch

- Dead Sea Scroll 11QpaleoLevᵃ: mlk (𐤉𐤋𐤌). Translation: king

- Leningrad Codex: Mōlek (מֹלֶךְ). Translation: Moloch

- Peshitta: nwkrytå (ܢܘܟܪܝܬܐ). Translation: (feminine) foreigners

- Targum Onkelos: Môlek (מוֹלֶךְ). Translation: Moloch

- Targum Jerusalem: Môlek (מוֹלֶךְ). Translation: Moloch

- Sahidic manuscript 2006: ark̆ōn (ⲁⲣⲭⲱⲛ). Translation: ruler

The meaning of this verse has been debated for thousands of years. The Greek translation treated the word as a human "ruler," suggesting a prohibition on sending one's children to fight for a ruler, presumably other than the king of Jerusalem. The Hebrew translation and the Aramaic Targum Onkelos both use the name Molech, which is believed to have been the Judahite variant of the Ammonite god Milcom, although this is still debated.

The Aramaic translations found in the Peshitta and Targum Jerusalem both read as prohibitions on interbreeding with non-Jews. As Leviticus was almost certainly written in Judahite, the precursor to Classical Hebrew, the original word would have been mlk (𐤉𐤋𐤌), meaning 'king,' as preserved in Dead Sea Scroll 11QpaleoLevᵃ. All records related to the translation indicate the Greek translation was made from an Aramaic translation, meaning the word would have been mlkå (ܢܝܠܟܐ), which means 'king' or 'ruler.' As the name Molech is likely the original term used in the verse, the common English translation of Moloch is used.

CHAPTER 21

Yahweh said to Moses, "Speak to the priests, the sons of Aaron, and you will tell them that they will not defile themselves in their nation for the dead, but they may mourn for a relative who is very near to them, for a father and mother, and sons and daughters, for a brother, and for a virgin sister that is near to one, that is not married to a man, for this one will defile himself. He will not defile himself suddenly among his people to profane himself."

"You will not shave your head for the dead with baldness on the top, and they will not shave their beard, nor will they cut gashes in their flesh. They will be holy to their god, and they will not profane the name of their god, for they offer the sacrifices of Yahweh as the gifts of their god, and they will be holy. They will not take a woman who is a harlot and profaned, or a woman put away from her husband. Holy is the lord of the gods. You will hallow him, he offers the gifts of Yahweh your God. He will be holy, for I, Yahweh that sanctify them, am holy. If the daughter of a priest should be profaned to go whoring, she profanes the name of her father, and she will be burnt with fire. The priest that is chief among his brothers, having had the oil poured on his head as the anointed one, and he having been consecrated to put on the garments, will not take the miter off his head, and will not rend his garments, neither will he go in to any dead body, neither will he defile himself for his father or his mother. He will not go forth out of the sanctuary, and he will not profane the sanctuary of his god, because the holy anointing oil of God is on him. I am Yahweh! He will take as a wife a virgin from his own tribe. But a widow, or one that is divorced, or profaned, or a harlot, these he will not take. He will take as a wife a virgin of his own people. He will not profane his seed among his people. I am Yahweh, who sanctifies him."

Yahweh said to Moses, "Tell Aaron, 'A man of your tribe throughout your generations, who has an imperfection in him, will not draw near to offer the gifts of his god. No man who has an imperfection in him will draw near, a man blind, lame, with a disfigured nose or his ears cut, a man who has a broken hand or a broken foot, or humpbacked, or blear-eyed, or that has lost his eye-lashes, or a man who has a malignant ulcer, or eczema, or one that has lost a testicle. Whoever is of the seed of Aaron the priest has an imperfection on him, will not come near to offer sacrifices to your god, because he has an imperfection on him. He will not come close and offer the gifts of god. The gifts of god are sacred, and he will eat of the holy things. Only he will not approach the veil, and he will not come close to the altar, because he has an imperfection, and he will not profane the sanctuary of his god, for I am Yahweh, who sanctifies them.'"

Moses spoke to Aaron and his sons, and all the children of Israel.

CHAPTER 22

Yahweh said to Moses, "Speak to Aaron and his sons, and let them pay attention concerning the holy things of the children of Israel, so they will not profane my holy name in any of the things which they consecrate to me. I am Yahweh!"

Say to them, "Every man throughout your generations, whoever from all your seed will approach the holy things, whatever the children of Israel will consecrate to Yahweh, while his uncleanness is on him, that mind will be cut off from me. I am the lord of the gods!"

"The man from the seed of Aaron the priest, if he should have leprosy or issue of the reins, will not eat of the holy things, until he is cleansed, and he that touches any uncleanness of a dead body, or the man whose semen has gone out from him, or whoever will touch any unclean reptile, which will defile him, or who will touch a man, whereby he will defile him according to all his uncleanness, whatever mind will touch them will be unclean until evening. He will not eat of the holy things unless he bathes his body in water, and the sun goes down, and then he will be clean, and then he will eat of all the holy things, for they are his bread. He will not eat that which dies itself or is taken from animals so that he should be polluted by them. I am Yahweh!"

"They will keep my ordinances, that they do not bear iniquity because of them, and die because of them if they profane them. I am Yahweh, the god who sanctifies them!"

"No foreigner will eat holy things. One who resides with a priest or an employee will not eat the holy things. But if a priest should have a slave purchased for silver, he will eat of his bread, and they that are born in his house, they also will eat of his bread. If the daughter of a priest should marry a stranger, she will not eat of the offerings of the sanctuary. If the daughter of a priest should be a widow, or divorced, and have no seed, she will return to her father's house, as in her youth. She will eat of her father's bread, but no stranger will eat it. The man who will ignorantly eat holy things will add the fifth part to it, and give the holy thing to the priest. They will not profane the holy things of the children of Israel, which they offer to Yahweh. So they should bring on themselves the iniquity of trespass in eating their holy things. I am the lord of the gods, the sanctifier of this!"[1]

Yahweh said to Moses, "Speak to Aaron and his sons, and all the congregation of Israel, and you will say to them, 'Any man of the children of Israel, or of the strangers that lives among them in Israel, who offers his gifts according to all their confession and according to all their choice, whatever they may bring to God whole burnt offerings your free will offerings will be males without imperfection of the herds, or the sheep, or the goats. They will not bring to Yahweh anything that has an imperfection in it, for it will not be acceptable for you. Whichever man will offer a peace-offering to Yahweh, discharging a vow, or in the way of free will offering, or an offering in your feasts, of the herds or of the sheep, it will be without imperfection for acceptance. There will be no imperfection in it. One that is blind, or broken, or has its tongue cut out, or is troubled with warts, or has a malignant ulcer, or eczema, they will not offer these to Yahweh. Nor will you offer any of them for a burnt offering on the altar of Yahweh. A calf or a sheep with the ears cut off, or that has lost its tail, you will kill them for yourself. But they will not be accepted for your vow. That which has broken testicles, or is crushed or gelded or mutilated, you will not offer them to Yahweh, nor will you sacrifice them on your land. Neither will you offer the gifts of your god of all these things by the hand of a stranger, because there is corruption in them, an imperfection in them. These will not be accepted for you."

Yahweh said to Moses, "As for a calf, or a sheep, or a goat, whenever it is born, then after it is seven days under its mother, and on the eighth day and after, they will be accepted for sacrifices, a burnt offering to Yahweh. A bullock and a ewe, it and its young, you will not kill in one day. If you should offer a sacrifice, a vow of rejoicing to Yahweh, you will offer it to be accepted for you. On that same day, it will be eaten. You will not leave some of the meat until the next day. I am Yahweh!

You will keep my commandments and do them. You will not profane the sacred name,[2] and I will be sanctified in the middle of the children of Israel. I am Yahweh, who sanctifies you, who brought you out of the land of Egypt, to be your god. I am Yahweh!'"

CHAPTER 22 NOTES

1 Codex Vaticanus: egō KS o agiazōn autous (ⲈⲄⲰ K̄C̄ Ⲟ ⲀⲄⲒⲀⲌⲰⲚⲀⲨⲦⲞⲨⲤ). Translation: I am Lord the sanctifier of this

• Codex Alexandrinus: egō KS o ṬS umōn o agiazōn autous (ⲈⲄⲰ K̄C̄Ⲟ̄Ⲑ̄C̄ⲨⲘⲰⲚⲞⲀⲄⲒⲀⲌⲰⲚⲀⲨⲦⲞⲨⲤ). Translation: I am Lord the god of y'all the sanctifier of this.

• Dead Sea Scroll 4QLev^b: ăny Yhwh mqdšm (אני יהוה מקדשם). Translation: I Yhwh of sanctuaries.

• Leningrad Codex: 'ănî Yəhwâ məqaddəšām (אֲנִי יְהוָה מְקַדְּשָׁם). Translation: I Yahweh of sanctuaries

• Peshitta: ănă ănă mryå dmqdš ănă lhwn (ܐܢܐ ܐܢܐ ܡܪܝܐ ܕܡܩܕܫ ܐܢܐ ܠܗܘܢ). Translation: I am master the temple (or sanctuary) I myself

• Targum Onkelos: tidḥal mē'ĕlāhāk 'ănā' yəyā (תִּדְחַל מֵאֱלָהָךְ אֲנָא יְיָ). Translation: be afraid of god of yours I'm Yh of sanctuaries

• Targum Jerusalem: 'ănā' Yəyā məqadišhôn (אֲנָא יְיָ מְקַדְשְׁהוֹן). Translation: I'm Yahweh of sacreds

• Sahidic manuscript 2006: ang ouhagios anok pjoeis eitbbo mmoou (ⲀⲚⲄ ⲞⲨ2ⲀⲄⲒⲞⲤ ⲀⲚⲞⲔ ⲠϪⲞⲈⲒⲤ ⲈⲒⲦⲂⲂⲞ ⲘⲘⲞⲞⲨ). Translation: I'm sacred one. I am the master who purifies the water

• Sahidic manuscript 2044: anok pe pjoeis ettbbo mmoou (ⲀⲚⲞⲔ ⲠⲈ ⲠϪⲞⲈⲒⲤ ⲈⲦⲦⲂⲂⲞ ⲘⲘⲞⲞⲨ). Translation: I am the master who purifies the water

• Sahidic manuscript 2047: ang ouhagios anok pjoeis pettbbo mmoou (ⲀⲚⲄ ⲞⲨ2ⲀⲄⲒⲞⲤ ⲀⲚⲞⲔ ⲠϪⲞⲈⲒⲤ ⲠⲈⲦⲦⲂⲂⲞ ⲘⲘⲰⲦⲚ).

CHAPTER 22

Translation: I'm sacred one. I am the master who purifies the all of them

This verse includes one of the two deviations between the Septuagint and Masoretic versions of Leviticus regarding the name of the author's god, assuming one accepts that Dead Sea Scroll 4QpapLXXLev[b] retains the original Greek translation of the Egypto-Aramaic Yåw (ⲓⲚ^) as Iaō (Ιαω). The Greek text indicates the Aramaic Text of Leviticus used the term 'ădōnāy hā'ĕlōhîm (אֲדֹנִי הָאֱלֹהִים), however, also restructured the verse slightly, likely because the Aramaic translator did not understand the Edomite word myqdšm (ⲨⲰⲀϤⲌⲨ).

2 Codex Vaticanus: to onoma tou agiou (**ΤΟ ΟΝΟΜΑ ΤΟΥ ΑΓΙΟΥ**). Translation: the name of sacred (or saint)

- LXX 19: to onoma to agion mou (ⲧⲟ Ⲫⲟμα ⲧⲟ ⲁⲅⲓⲱ μⲟⲩ).
Translation: the name of sacred (or saint) of me
- LXX 44: to onoma to agion (ⲧⲟ Ⲫⲟμα ⲧⲟ ⲁⲅⲓⲱ). Translation: the name of sacred (or saint)
- LXX 55: to onoma tou agiou auta (ⲧⲟ Ⲫⲟμα ⲧⲱ ⲁⲅⲓⲟⲩ ⲁⲩⲧⲁ). Translation: the name of sacred (or saint) mine
- LXX 58: to onoma to agion mou egō KS (ⲧⲟ Ⲫⲟμα ⲧⲟ ⲁⲅⲓⲱ μⲟⲩ ⲟⲅⲱ ⲔⲤ). Translation: the name of sacred (or saint) mine I'm Lord
- LXX 75: to onoma agiasthēsōmai (ⲧⲟ Ⲫⲟμα ⲁⲅⲓⲁⲟⲑⲏⳠⲱμⲁⲩ). Translation: the name Agiasthēsōmai
- LXX 134: to onoma mou to agiou egō KS (ⲧⲟ Ⲫⲟμα μⲟⲩ ⲧⲟ ⲁⲅⲓⲟⲩ ⲟⲅⲱ ⲔⲤ). Translation: the name mine of sacred (or saint) I'm Lord

CHAPTER 22

- Leningrad Codex: 'et-šēm qodšî (אֶת־שֵׁם קָדְשִׁי). Translation: the name sacred (or Qetesh)
- Peshitta: šmå dqwdšy (ܫܡܐ ܕܩܘܕܫܝ). Translation: name of Qetesh (or sacred)
- Targum Onkelos: 'ănā' yəyā məqaddiškôn (אֲנָא יְיָ מְקַדִּשְׁכוֹן). Translation: I'm Yahweh of sacredness
- Sahidic manuscript 2006: mpran mppetuaab (ⲙⲡⲣⲁⲛ ⲙⲡⲡⲉⲧⲟⲩⲁⲁⲃ). Translation: the name of the sacred

CHAPTER 23

Yahweh said to Moses, "Speak to the children of Israel, and you will say to them, 'The feasts of Yahweh, which you will call holy assemblies, these are my feasts. Six days you will do work, but on the seventh day is the sabbath, a rest, a holy convocation to Yahweh. You will not do any work, it is a sabbath to Yahweh in all your dwellings. These are the feasts to Yahweh, holy assemblies which you will call in their seasons. In the first month, on the fourteenth day of the month, between the evening times is Yahweh's Passover. On the fifteenth day of this month is the feast of unleavened bread for Yahweh, and for seven days will you eat unleavened bread."

"The first day will be a holy convocation to you, and you will do no servile work. You will offer whole burnt offerings to Yahweh for seven days, and the seventh day will be a holy convocation to you, and you will do no servile work."

Yahweh said to Moses, "Tell the children of Israel, 'When you will enter into the land which I give you, and reap the harvest it, then will you bring a sheaf, the first fruits of your harvest, to the priest, and he will lift the sheaf before Yahweh, to be accepted for you. On the morning of the first day, the priest will lift it. You will offer on the day on which you bring the sheaf, a lamb without imperfection of a year old for a whole burnt offering to Yahweh. It's meat-offering two tenth portions of fine flour mingled with oil: it is a sacrifice to

Yahweh, a smell of sweet savor to Yahweh, and its drink-offering a quarter of a hin[1] of wine. You will not eat bread, or the new parched grain, until this same day, until you offer the sacrifices to your god. It is a perpetual statute throughout your generations in all your dwellings.'"

"'You will count for yourselves from the day after the sabbath, from the day on which you will offer the sheaf of the heave-offering, seven full weeks until the morning after the last week you will count fifty days and will bring a new meat-offering to Yahweh. You will bring from your dwelling loaves, as a heave-offering, two loaves, they will be of two tenth portions of fine flour, they will be baked with the leaven of the first fruits for Yahweh. You will bring with the loaves seven undamaged lambs, each a year old, and one calf of the herd, and two rams without imperfection, and they will be a whole burnt offering to Yahweh. Their meat-offerings and their drink-offerings will be a sacrifice, a smell of sweet savor to Yahweh. They will sacrifice one kid of the goats for a sin-offering, and two lambs, each a year old, for a peace-offering, with the loaves of the first fruits.'"

"'The priest will place them with the loaves of the first-fruits, and offering before Yahweh with the two lambs, they will be holy to Yahweh. They will belong to the priest who brings them. You will call this day a convocation. It will be holy to you. You will do no servile work on it. It is a perpetual ordinance throughout your generations in all your habitations. When you reap the harvest of your land, you will not fully reap the remainder of the harvest of your field when you reap, and you will not gather that which falls from your reaping. You will leave it for the poor and the stranger. I am Yahweh, your god!'"

Yahweh said to Moses, "Tell the children of Israel, 'In the seventh month, on the first day of the month, you will rest with a celebration of trumpets. It will be a holiday for you. You will do no servile work, and you will offer a whole burnt offering to Yahweh.'"

Yahweh said to Moses, "Also on the tenth day of this seventh month is a day of atonement. It will be a holy convocation to you, and you will humble your minds, and offer a whole burnt offering to Yahweh. You will do no work on this day, for this is a day of atonement for you, to make atonement for you before Yahweh your god. Every mind that will not be humbled in that day, will be cut off from among its people. Every mind that does work on that day, that mind will be destroyed from among its people. You will do no manner of work: it is a perpetual statute throughout your generations in all your habitations. It will be a holy sabbath to you, and you will humble your minds, from the ninth day of the month: from evening to evening you will keep your sabbaths."

Yahweh said to Moses, "Tell the children of Israel, 'On the fifteenth day of this seventh month, there will be a feast of tabernacles seven days to Yahweh. On the first day will be a holy convocation, and you will do no servile work. Seven days will you offer whole burnt offerings to Yahweh, and the eighth day will be a holy convocation to you, and you will offer whole burnt offerings to Yahweh. It is a time of release; you will do no servile work. These are the feasts to Yahweh, which you will call holy assemblies, to offer burnt offerings to Yahweh, whole burnt offerings, and their meat-offerings, and their drink-offerings, that for each day on its day. Besides the sabbaths of Yahweh, and your gifts, and all your vows, and your freewill offerings, which you will give to Yahweh, on the fifteenth day of this seventh month, when you have completely gathered in the fruits of the land, you will keep a feast to Yahweh seven days. On the first day, there will be a rest, and on the eighth day, a rest. On the first day, you will take good fruit from trees, and branches of palm trees, and thick boughs of trees, and willows, and branches of osiers from the brook, to rejoice before Yahweh your God seven days in the year. It is a perpetual statute for your generations. In the seventh month, you will keep it. Seven days you will dwell in tabernacles: every native in Israel will dwell in tents, that your posterity may see, that I made the children of Israel dwell in tents when I brought them out of the land of Egypt. I am the lord of the gods!"

So Moses recounted the feasts of Yahweh to the children of Israel.

Chapter 23 Notes

1 Codex Vaticanus: in (ιν)
- LXX 58: ein (ϟν)

CHAPTER 23

- Leningrad Codex: hîn (הִין)
- Peshitta: hmynå (ܗܡܝܢܐ). Translation: belt (a unit of measurement in the Persian empire)
- Targum Onkelos: hina (הִינָא)
- Targum Jerusalem: hina (הִינָא)
- Sahidic manuscript 2006: hin (ϩⲓⲛ)

The hin was ancient Samaritan and Judahite unit of measurement estimated around 3.7 liters (3.9 quarts).

CHAPTER 24

Yahweh said to Moses, "Order the children of Israel and let them take for you pure beaten olive oil for the light, to burn a lamp continually, outside the veil in the tabernacle of witness, and Aaron and his sons will burn it from evening until morning before Yahweh continually, a perpetual statute throughout your generations. You will burn the lamps on the pure lamp-stand before Yahweh until the morning. You will take fine flour, and make it twelve loaves; each loaf will be of two-tenths parts. You will put them in two rows, each row containing six loaves, on the pure table before Yahweh. You will put in each row pure frankincense and salt, and these things will be for loaves for a memorial, set out before Yahweh."

"On the sabbath-day, they will be set out before Yahweh continually before the children of Israel, for an eternal covenant. They will be for Aaron and his sons, and they will eat them in the holy place. For this is their sacred portion of the offerings made to Yahweh, a perpetual statute."

There was a son of an Israelite woman, and he was the son of an Egyptian man among the sons of Israel, and they fought in the camp, the son of the Israelite woman, and a man who was an Israelite. The son of the Israelite woman was cursed by the name, and they brought him to Moses. His mother's name was Salomith, daughter of Dabri of the tribe of Dan. They held him in a ward to judge him by the command of Yahweh.

CHAPTER 24

Yahweh said to Moses, "Bring him out who cursed outside the camp, and all who heard will lay their hands on his head, and all the congregation will stone him. Speak to the sons of Israel, and you will say to them, 'Whoever will curse God will bear his sin. He that names the name of Yahweh, let him die the death. Let all the congregation of Israel stone him with stones, whether he is a stranger or a native, let him die for cursing the name of Yahweh."

"Whoever strikes a man and he dies, let him die the death."

"Whoever will strike an animal, and it will die, let him return life for life."

"Whoever will inflict an imperfection on his neighbor, as he has done to him, so will it be done to himself in return: bruise for bruise, eye for eye, tooth for tooth."

"If anyone inflicts an imperfection on a man, so will it be rendered to him."

"Whoever will strike a man, and he will die, let him die the death."

"There will be one judgment for the stranger and the native, for I am Yahweh your God!"

Moses spoke to the children of Israel, and they brought him who had cursed out of the camp, and stoned him with stones. The children of Israel did as Yahweh commanded Moses.

CHAPTER 25

Yahweh spoke to Moses on Mount Sinai, saying, "Tell the children of Israel, "Whenever you have entered into the land, which I give to you, then the land will rest which I give to you, for its sabbaths to Yahweh. Six years you will sow your field, and six years you will prune your vine, and gather in its fruit. But in the seventh year will be a sabbath, it will be a rest to the land, a sabbath to Yahweh. You will not sow your field, and you will not prune your vine. You will not gather the spontaneous produce of your field, and you will not fully gather the grapes of your dedication. It will be a year of rest for the land. The sabbaths of the land will be food for you, and for your man-slave, and your woman-slave, and your employee, and the stranger that lives with you. For your livestock, and for the wild beasts that are in your land, will every fruit be for food."

"You will calculate for yourself seven sabbaths of years, seven times seven years, and they will be for you seven weeks of years, forty-nine years. In the seventh month, on the tenth day of the month, you will proclaim with the sound of a trumpet in all your land. On the day of atonement, you will proclaim with a trumpet in all your land. You will sanctify the year, the fiftieth year, and you will proclaim a release on the land for all that inhabit it. It will be given a year of release, a jubilee for you, and each one will depart to his possession, and you will go each to his family. This is a jubilee of release, the year will be for you the fiftieth year, you will not sow, nor reap the produce that comes itself from the land, nor will you gather its planted fruits. It is a jubilee of release. It will be holy to you, you will eat its fruit of the fields."

"In the year of the release, the jubilee, will each one return to his possession. If you should sell a possession to your neighbor, or if you should buy from your neighbor, don't let a man oppress his neighbor. According to the number of years after the jubilee, you will buy from your neighbor, according to the number of years the fruits will he sold to you. If it is a greater number of years, he will increase the value of his possession, and if there is a smaller number of years, he will decrease the value of his possession, according to the number of crops, so will he sell to you. Don't let a man oppress his neighbor, and you will fear Yahweh your god. I am Yahweh, your god!"

"You will keep all my ordinances, and all my judgments, and observe them, and you will keep them, and dwell securely in the land. The land will yield her increase, and you will eat to fullness and will dwell securely in it. If you should say, 'What will we eat in this seventh year, if we do not sow nor gather in our fruits?' Then will I send my blessing on you in the sixth year, and the land will produce enough fruits for three years. You will sow in the eighth year, and eat old fruits until the ninth year: until its fruit comes, you will eat old fruits of the old. The land will not be sold permanently, as the land is mine, and because you were strangers and travelers before me. In every land of your possession, you will allow ransoms for the land. If your brother who is with you is poor, and should have sold part of his possession, and his relative who is near to him comes, then he will redeem the possession which his brother has sold. If one has no nearby relative, and he prospers with his hand, and he finds sufficient silver, enough for his ransom, then he will calculate the years of his sale, and he will give what is due to the man to whom he sold it, and he will return to his possession. But if his hand has not prospered sufficiently, so that he could restore the silver to him, then he who bought the possessions has them until the sixth year of the release, and it will go out in the release, and the owner will return to his possession. If anyone should sell an inhabited house in a walled city, then there will be a ransom on it, until the time is fulfilled. Its time of ransom will be a full year. If it isn't ransomed within a complete year, the house which is in the walled city will surely be confirmed to him who bought it, throughout his generations, and it will not go out in the release. But the houses in the villages that have no walls around them will be considered as the fields of the country. They will always be redeemable, and they will go out in the release.

The cities of the Levites, the houses of the cities in their possession, will always be redeemable to the Levites. If anyone will redeem a house of the Levites, then their purchase of the houses of their possession goes out in the release, because the houses of the cities of the Levites are their possession among the children of Israel. The lands set apart for their cities will not be sold, because this is their perpetual possession."

"If your brother who is with you becomes poor, and he fails in resources with you, you will help him as a stranger and a traveler, and your brother will live with you. You will not charge him interest, nor increase, and you will fear your god. I am Yahweh! Your brother will live with you. You will not lend your silver to him at interest, and you will not lend your meat to him to be returned with an increase. I am Yahweh, your God, who brought you out of the land of Egypt, to give you the land of Canaan, to be your God!"

If your brother near you is lowered, and is sold to you, he will not serve you with the servitude of a slave. He will be with you as an employee or a traveler. He will work for you until the year of release, and he will go out in the release, and his children with him, and he will go to his family, and he will rush back to his patrimony. Because these are my servants, whom I brought out of the land of Egypt, they will not be sold like a common slave. You will not oppress him with labor, and will fear Yahweh, your god. However many men-slaves and woman-slaves you have, you will purchase your male and female slaves from the nations that are around you. Of the sons of the travelers that are among you, from these you will buy and of their relations, all that will be in your lands. Let them be a possession for you. You will distribute them to your children after you, and they will be your permanent possessions forever. As to your brothers, the children of Israel, you will not oppress your brother with labor."

"If a stranger or traveler with you becomes rich, and your brother in distress is sold to the stranger or the traveler that is with you, or to a proselyte by extraction; after he is sold to him, there will be redemption for him. One of his brothers will redeem him. A brother of his father or a son of his father's brother will redeem him, or let one of his near family of his tribe redeem him. If he should become rich and redeem himself, then he will calculate with his purchaser from the year that he sold himself to him until the year of release, and the silver of his purchase will be as that of an employee; he will be with him from year to year. If any have a greater number of years than enough, according to these, he will pay his ransom out of his purchase-silver. If but a little time is left of the years until the year of release, then he will consider him according to his years and will pay his wages as an employee. He will be with him from year to year. You will not oppress him with labor before you. If he does not pay his ransom accordingly, he will go out in the year of his release, he and his children with him. The children of Israel are my servants. They are my attendants, whom I brought out of the land of Egypt."

CHAPTER 26

"I am Yahweh, your god! You will not make for yourselves gods made with hands or engraved. Nor will you set up a stele[1] for yourselves, nor will you set up a stone for an object in your land to worship it. I am the lord of the gods!"

"You will keep my sabbaths, and revere my sanctuaries: I am Yahweh! If you follow my ordinances, and keep my commandments, and do them, then I will give you the rain in its season, and the land will produce its fruits, and the trees of the field will yield their fruit. Your threshing time will surpass the vintage, and your vintage will surpass your seed time, and you will eat your bread to the full, and you will dwell safely on your land, and war will not go through your land. I will give peace in your land, and you will sleep, and none will make you afraid. I will destroy the evil animals out of your land, and you will chase your enemies, and they will fall before you in slaughter."

"Five of you will chase a hundred, and a hundred of you will chase tens of thousands, and your enemies will fall before you by the sword. I will look on you, and increase you, and multiply you, and establish my covenant with you. You will consume that which is old and very old, and drive out the old to make way for the new. I will set my tabernacle among you, and my mind will not hate you, and I will walk among you, and be your god, and you will be my people."

CHAPTER 26

"I am Yahweh, your God, who brought you out of the land of Egypt, where you were slaves, and I broke the bands of your shackles, and brought you out openly. But if you will not listen to me, nor obey these my ordinances, but disobey them, and your mind should loathe my judgments, so that you should not keep all my commands, to break my covenant, then I will do this to you: I will even bring on you perplexity and the itch, and the fever that causes your eyes to waste away, and disease that consumes your life, and you will sow your seeds in vain, and your enemies will eat them. I will set my face against you, and you will fall before your enemies, and they who hate you will chase you, and you will flee with no one pursuing you. If you still refuse to listen to me, then I will punish you another seven times for your sins. I will break down the haughtiness of your pride, and I will make your sky like iron, and your land like brass."

"Your strength will be in vain, and your land will not yield its seed, and the tree of your field will not yield its fruit. If, after this, you should walk perversely, and not be willing to obey me, I will further bring on you seven plagues according to your sins. I will send against you the wild animals of the land, and they will devour you and will consume your livestock, and I will make you few in number, and your roads will be desolate. If subsequently you are not corrected but walk perversely towards me, I also will walk with you with a perverse spirit, and I also will strike you seven times for your sins. I will bring on you a sword avenging the cause of my covenant, and you will flee for refuge to your cities, and I will send out death against you, and you will be delivered into the hands of your enemies. When I afflict you with a famine of bread, then ten women will bake your loaves in one oven, and they will render your loaves by weight, and you will eat, and not be satisfied. If, after this, you will not obey me, but walk perversely towards me, then I will walk with you with a prepared mind, and I will punish you seven times, according to your sins. You will eat the flesh of your sons, and the flesh of your daughters you will eat."

"I will render your steles desolate, and will utterly destroy your wooden images made with hands, and I will lay your carcasses on the carcasses of your idols, and my mind will loathe you. I will lay your cities waste, and I will make your sanctuaries desolate, and I will not smell the savor of your sacrifices. I will lay your land desolate, and your enemies who dwell in it will wonder at it. I will scatter you among the nations, and the sword will come on you and consume you, and your land will be desolate, and your cities will be desolate. Then the land will enjoy its sabbaths all the days of its desolation. You will be in the land of your enemies; then the land will keep its sabbaths, and the land will enjoy its sabbaths all the days of its desolation: it will keep sabbaths which it kept not among your sabbaths when you lived in it. To those who are left of you, I will bring slavery into their heart in the land of their enemies, and the sound of a shaken leaf will chase them, and they will flee as fleeing from war and will fall when none pursues them. Brother will disregard brother, as in war, when no one pursues, and you will not be able to withstand your enemies. You will perish among the Gentiles, and the land of your enemies will devour you. Those who are left of you will perish, because of their sins, and because of the sins of their fathers: in the land of their enemies will they consume away. They will confess their sins, and the sins of their fathers, that they have transgressed and neglected me, and that they have walked perversely before me, and I walked with them with a perverse mind, and I will destroy them in the land of their enemies. Then their uncircumcised heart will be ashamed, and then they will acquiesce in the punishment of their sins."

"I will remember the covenant of Jacob, and the covenant of Isaac, and the covenant of Abraham, I will also remember. I will remember the land, and the land will be left of them; then the land will enjoy her sabbaths when it is deserted through them: and they will accept the punishment of their iniquities, because they neglected my judgments, and in their mind loathed my ordinances. Yet not even thus, while they were in the land of their enemies, did I overlook them, nor did I loathe them to consume them, to break my covenant made with them, for I am Yahweh their god. I will remember their former covenant, when I brought them out of the land of Egypt, out of the house of slavery, before the nation, to be their God. I am Yahweh!"

These are my judgments and my ordinances, and the law which Yahweh gave between himself and the children of Israel, in Mount Sinai, by the hand of Moses.

CHAPTER 26

CHAPTER 26 NOTES

1 Codex Vaticanus: stēlēn (ϹΤΗΛΗΝ). Translation: stele (or pillar)

• Leningrad Codex: maṣṣēbâ (מַצֵּבָה). Translation: pillar (or monument, tree-stump)

• Peshitta: qymtå (ܩܝܡܬܐ). Translation: columns (or statues, tree trunks, necromancy, resurrection)

• Targum Onkelos: ṣelem (צְלֵם). Translation: idols

• Fragment Targums: 'eben diṭ'û (אֶבֶן דִּטְעוּ). Translation: stone misleading (or idol)

• Targum Jerusalem: ṣîləmîn (צִילְמִין). Translation: statue

• Vetus Latina manuscripts: titulus (ΤΙΤϹLϹS). Translation: inscription (or epitaph)

• Liber de divinis scripturis sive Speculum: stantes lapide (ЅΤΛΝΤƐЅ LΛΡΙϦƐ). Translation: standing stone (or grave stone, statue)

• Sahidic manuscript 2006: stēlē (ϹΤΗΛΗ). Translation: stele (or pillar)

CHAPTER 27

Yahweh said to Moses, "Tell the children of Israel, 'Whoever will vow a vow as the value of his mind for Yahweh, the value of a male from twenty years old to sixty years old will be his value, which will be fifty shekels of silver[1] by the standard of the sanctuary. The value of a female will be thirty shekels. If it is from five years old to twenty, the value of a male will be twenty shekels, and of a female ten shekels. From a month old to five years old, the value of a male will be five shekels, and of a female, three shekels of silver. If from sixty years old and upward, if it is a male, his value will be fifteen shekels of silver, and if a female, ten shekels. If the man is too poor for the value, he will stand before the priest, and the priest will value him: according to what the man who has vowed can afford, the priest will value him.'"

"If it is from the livestock that is offered as a gift to Yahweh, whoever will offer one of these to Yahweh, it will be holy. He will not change it, a good for a bad, or a bad for a good, and if he does at all change it, an animal for an animal, it and the substitute will be holy. If it is any unclean animal, of which none are offered as a gift to Yahweh, he will set the animal before the priest. The priest will make a value between the good and the bad, and accordingly, as the priest values it, so will it stand. If the worshiper will at all redeem it, he will add the fifth part to its value. Whatever man will consecrate his house as holy to Yahweh, the priest will make an evaluation of it between the good and the bad. As the priest will value it, so will it stand. If he that has sanctified it should redeem his house, he will add to it the fifth part of the silver of the value, and it will be his."

"If a man should offer to Yahweh a part of the field of his possession, then the value will be according to its seed, fifty shekels of silver for a kor[2] of barley. If he should sanctify his field from the year of release, it will stand according to its value. If he should sanctify his field in the latter time after the release, the priest will reckon to him the silver for the remaining years, until the next year of release, and it will be deducted as an equivalent from his full value. If he who sanctified the field would redeem it, he would add to its value the fifth part of the silver, and it would be his. If he does not redeem the field but sells the field to another man, he will not be able to redeem it. But the field will be holy to Yahweh after the release, as a separated land, the priest will possess it. If he should consecrate to Yahweh a field which he has bought, which is not of the field of his possession, the priest will reckon to him the full value from the year of release, and he will pay the value on that day as holy to Yahweh.

"In the year of release, the land will be restored to the man of whom the other bought it, whose possession of the land was. Every value will be by holy weights: the shekel will be twenty gerahs.[3] Every firstborn that will be produced among your livestock will be Yahweh's, and no man will sanctify it, whether calf or sheep, it is Yahweh's. But if he should redeem an unclean animal, according to its value, then he will add the fifth part to it, and it will be his, and if he does not redeem it, it will be sold according to its value. Every dedicated thing which a man will dedicate to Yahweh of all that he has, whether man or animal, or of the field of his possession, he will not sell it, nor redeem it. Every devoted thing will be sacred to Yahweh. Whatever will be dedicated to men, will not be ransomed, but will be surely put to death. Every tithe of the land, both of the seed of the land, and the fruit of trees, is Yahweh's; it is holy to Yahweh. If a man should at all redeem his tithe, he will add the fifth part to it, and it will be his. Every tithe of oxen, and sheep, and whatever may be counted under the wand, the tenth will be holy to Yahweh. You will not change a good for a bad, or a bad for a good, and if you should at all change it, its equivalent also will be holy, it will not be redeemed."

These are the commandments that Yahweh commanded Moses for the sons of Israel on Mount Sinai.

CHAPTER 27 NOTES

1 Codex Vaticanus: didrachma arguriou (ΔΙΔΡΑΧΜΑ ΑΡΓΥΡΙΟΥ). Translation: two-drachmas silver

• Codex Ambrosiano A 147: didragma (ΔΙΔΡΑΓΜΑ). Translation: two-drachmas

• Leningrad Codex: šəqālîm (שְׁקָלִים). Translation: shekels

• Peshitta: mtqlyn (ܡܬܩܠܝܢ). Translation: scales (or weight, shekel, beka)

- Targum Onkelos: sil'în (סִלְעִין). Translation: selas (or rocks)
- Targum Jerusalem: sil'în (סִלְעִין). Translation: selas (or rocks)
- Vetus Latina manuscripts: argenti didragchima (ARCENTI ƆIƆR ACCΠIƆA). Translation: silver didracchima
- Sahidic manuscript 2006: timē (TIMH). Translation: money (or profit)

The shekel was a unit of weight used throughout the Middle East for thousands of years, weighing approximately 8.6 grams of silver. The Greek drachma was a coin weighing approximately half a shekel, and therefore, under Greek rule of the Middle East, a two-drachma coin was used. As the Greeks clearly translated shekel into didrachma, the term shekel is restored in this translation. The sela, mentioned in the Targums, was a weight and coin, although the value varied depending on the metal it was made from.

2 Codex Vaticanus: korou (ΚΟΡΟΥ)
- LXX 53: koron (ΚΟΡΟΝ)
- LXX 75: koros (ΚΟΡΟϹ)
- DSS 11QpaleoLevᵃ: hmr (𐤇𐤌𐤓)
- Leningrad Codex: hōmer (חֹמֶר)
- Peshitta: kwr (ܟܘܪ)
- Targum Onkelos: kûr (כּוֹר)
- Targum Jerusalem II: hômer (חוֹמֶר)
- Targum Jerusalem: kôr (כּוֹר)
- Vetus Latina manuscripts: modioru (ƆOƆIORU)
- Sahidic manuscript 2006: ši (ϣI). Translation: measurement of area or volume

The Greek and Hebrew translations use different units of measurement which are considered equivalents in different languages. The Septuagint uses a transliteration of the Imperial

CHAPTER 27

Aramaic word kwrå (עֲיָרָא), which was also the precursor to the
Syriac word kwr (ܟܘܪ) in the Peshitta, kûr (כּוּר) in the Targum
Onkelos, and kôr (כּוֹר) in the Targum Jerusalem. It referred to the
ancient Mesopotamian unit of measurement known as the kurru
(𒄢). The Masoretic text includes a direct transliteration of the
Phoenician spelling of the word ḥmr (𐤇𐤌𐤓), the Canaanite
equivalent of the kurru, which was also the term used in the
Samaritan Dead Sea Scroll 11QpaleoLevᵃ from the Herodian dynasty.
The existence of the Canaanite word confirms the text of *Leviticus*
was almost certainly written in Judahite before the rise of the Neo-
Babylonian Empire.

3 Codex Vaticanus: oboloe (ΟΒΟΛΟΙ). Translation: obols

- LXX 71: tō kuríō (Τοο ΚυΡϕοο). Translation: to lord

- LXX 129: obolois (ΟΙΙΟ/ΟΙΣ). Translation: obol

- Leningrad Codex: gerah (גֵּרָה)

- Peshitta: môyn (ܡܥܝܢ). Translations: m'ahs

- Targum Onkelos: ma'in (מָעִין). Translations: m'ahs

- Targum Jerusalem: ma'in (מָעִין). Translations: m'ahs

- Vetus Latina manuscripts: Dni (ΟΝΙ). Translation: denarii

- Sahidic manuscript 2006: obolos (ΟΒΟΛΟϹ)

The obol was a Greek coin used from around 1100 BCE, worth ⅙
of a drachma, approximately 0.72 grams of silver. The gerah was a
measurement equaling one-twentieth of a shekel. The mina
mentioned in the Peshitta and Targum Onkelos was an ancient
Mesopotamian coin and measurement; however, it was much larger
than the shekel, generally valued at 60 shekels. As the Greek
translation translates the name of the measurement to obol, the
name gerah is restored in this translation. The Old Latin translators

substituted the softened plural form of denarius, a Roman coin in circulation between 211 BCE and 244 CE.

Septuagint Manuscripts

The following is a list of the Septuagint manuscripts referenced in the notes for this book.

LXX A (Codex Alexandrinus) is dated to the 5th century. It is currently located at the British Library (Royal 1 D. VIII) in London.

LXX B (Codex Vaticanus) is dated to the 4th century. It is currently located at the Vatican Library (Gr. 1209) in Vatican City.

LXX G (Codex Colberto-Sarravianus) is dated to the 4th or 5th century. Sections of it are currently located at the University Library (Voss. graec. in qu. 8) in Leiden, the French National Library (Grec 17) in Paris, and the Russian National Library (Gr. 3) in St. Petersburg.

LXX 44 is dated to the 15th century. It is currently located at the Stadtbibliothek (A 1) in Zittau.

LXX 55 is dated to the 10th century. It is currently located at the Vatican Library (Regin. Gr. 1) in Vatican City.

LXX 58 is dated to the 11th century. It is currently located at the Vatican Library (Regin. gr. 10) in Vatican City.

LXX 72 is dated to the 13th century. It is currently located at the Bodleian Library (Canonic. Gr. 35) in Oxford.

LXX 75 is dated to 1125. It is currently located at University College (52) in Oxford.

LXX 106 is dated to the 14th century. It is currently located at the Biblioteca Comunale Ariostea (187 I-III) in Ferrara.

LXX 134 is dated to the 11th century. It is currently located at the Biblioteca Marciana (Plut. 5.1) in Venice.

Septuagint Manuscripts

LXX 802 (4QpapLXXLev^b) is dated to the 1st century BCE. It is currently located at the Rockefeller Museum (4Q120) in Jerusalem. This document is also known as Dead Sea Scroll 4Q120.

ALTERNATIVE SOURCES

The following is a list of alternative translations that were used for comparative analysis. Both the Peshitta and Coptic translations are believed to have been heavily based on the Septuagint, although they do inherit relics of older Imperial Aramaic translations or imports from the Hebrew translation.

The Leningrad Codex is dated to 1008 (or 1009) CE. It is currently located at the National Library of Russia (Firkovich B 19 A) in St. Petersburg. The Leningrad Codex is the oldest complete copy of the Hebrew scriptures used within Judaism.

The Peshitta is the Classical Syriac Aramaic translation of the Christian bible. The Old Testament was translated from older Aramaic and Hebrew sources during the late 2nd century CE.

The Targum Onkelos is generally accepted as having been compiled by Aquila (Onkelos) of Sinope between 100 and 120 CE, although the surviving copies are all in Babylonian Aramaic, and the text appears to have been updated linguistically in Babylon in the 4th or 5th centuries CE. Some scholars believe Aquila was reworking a now lost, older Judean-Aramaic targum from the 1st century. The Megillah (3a) tractate of the Babylonian Torah claims that the Onkelos Targum is a restoration of a version of the Torah in use before the time of Ezra the scribe in the 4th century BCE. While the idea that Aquila and Onkelos were the same person, the Talmuds mention both of them doing the same thing, creating a targum in the same era, but do not confirm that they are the same person. Therefore, the Onkelos is sometimes viewed as being a continuation of an older Babylonian Aramaic translation from the Neo-Babylonian, Persian, or Greek eras.

The Targum Pseudo-Jonathan has historically been misidentified as the Targum Jonathan, and is also called the Targum Jerusalem in some literature, although this is not the same document as the

Targum Jerusalem listed below. It is written in Palestinian-Aramaic, and generally dated to sometime between the 4th and 11th centuries. Some scholars believe it originated in the 4th century and was modified after the Islamic conquest of Palestine, as it includes some Arabic names generally found in Islamic sources. It existed before the crusades, as it was documented at the time.

The Targum Jerusalem, sometimes called the Targum Jerusalem II or the Fragments Targum, is a collection of fragments from one or more targums written in Judean Aramaic that surfaced in Italy during the medieval era. It contains a number of heretical concepts, such as Judean-polytheism, suggesting some are a relic of a polytheist Israelite sect from before the Maccabean Revolt. The oldest Targum Jerusalem fragments date to the medieval period or later, and are copies of a manuscript reworked in the 5th century CE. However, the Targum is written in a form of Judeo-Aramaic that supports its origin in the Persian, Hellenistic, or Hasmonean eras.

The Vetus Latina manuscripts are Old Latin manuscripts translated from Aramaic and Greek sources between the 3rd century BCE and 4th century CE. Surviving manuscripts are copies that were made much later. The earliest surviving manuscripts that include *Leviticus* date to the 5th century CE.

The *Liber de divinis scripturis sive Speculum* is a Latin commentary on the Christian scriptures from the Medieval era, once attributed to Augustine of Hippo. Its origin is unclear; however, the quotes it cites are often different from known Old Latina manuscripts, and it is generally believed that the author was translating his quotes from another language.

The Coptic manuscripts are translations of the Septuagint into Coptic, the Classical form of Egyptian. Translations of the Septuagint were made into at least five of the Coptic dialects, however, complete copies only survive in Bohairic and Sahidic. These dialects were written slightly differently, and therefore words transliterated into Coptic retain slightly different pronunciations, reflecting the different source texts used.

Sahidic manuscripts are translations of the Septuagint into Sahidic (also known as Thebaic), one of the six dialects of Coptic, the classical era form of the Egyptian language. Sahidic was the dominant form of Coptic used before the 11th century, and is believed to have originated in the region around Hermopolis, at the boundary between Upper and Lower Egypt. Translations of the Septuagint into Sahidic are known to have existed by the 4th century, however, early non-dialect specific translations are generally accepted as having been made as early as the 1st century CE, with some scholars suggesting the 1st century BCE. The early non-dialect specific forms of Coptic are generally grouped with Sahidic, as Sahidic did not have a standardized spelling until the 6th century.

Sahidic manuscript 2006 is dated to the 9th or 10th century. It is currently located at the Morgan Library & Museum (M 566) in New York City.

Sahidic manuscript 2044 is dated to the 7th century. It is currently located at the Institut Français d'Archéologie Orientale (Inv. no. 215A) in Cairo.

Sahidic manuscript 2047 is dated to the 10th century. It is currently located at the Universitätsbibliothek Leuven (Copt. Lov. 3) in Leuven, in the Staatsbibliothek zu Berlin Preußischer Kulturbesitz (Ms. or. fol. 1605, Blatt 2) in Berlin, in the Bibliothèque nationale de France (Copte 129, Copte 132) in Paris, the University Library (Or. 16.1699 Π ii) in Cambridge, the British Library (Or. 3579 A) in London, the Österreichische Nationalbibliothek (K 9387) in Vienna, and the Biblioteca Apostolica Vaticana (Borg. Copt. 109).

DEAD SEA SCROLLS

The following is a list of the Dead Sea Scrolls mentioned in the notes for this book. Most are held by the Israel Museum in Jerusalem.

DSS 1Q3 (1QpaleoLev) is dated to the Roman rule of Judea and Palestine (6 to 390 CE).

DSS 4Q23 (4QLev-Num^a) is dated to the Hasmonean Dynasty in Judea (140 to 37 BCE).

DSS 4Q24 (4QLev^b) is dated to the Hasmonean Dynasty in Judea (140 to 37 BCE).

DSS 4Q25 (4QLev^c) is dated to the Roman rule of Judea and Palestine (6 to 390 CE).

DSS 4Q26 (4QLev^d) is dated to the Roman rule of Judea and Palestine (6 to 390 CE).

DSS 4Q26a (4QLev^e) is dated to the Roman rule of Judea and Palestine (6 to 390 CE).

DSS 4Q26b (4QLev^g) is dated to the Roman rule of Judea and Palestine (6 to 390 CE).

DSS 4Q120 (4QpapLXXLev^b) is dated to the Hasmonean Dynasty in Judea (140 to 37 BCE). This document is also known as LXX 802.

DSS 6Q2 (6QpaleoLev) is dated to the Greek rule of Judea (330 to 140 CE).

DSS 11Q1 (11QpaleoLev^a) is dated to the Herodian Dynasty in Judea (37 BCE to 6 CE).

DSS 11Q2 (11QLev^b) is dated to the Herodian Dynasty in Judea (37 BCE to 6 CE).

DSS Mas1a (MasLev[a]) is dated to the Roman rule of Judea and Palestine (6 to 390 CE).

DSS Mas1b (MasLev[b]) is dated to the Roman rule of Judea and Palestine (6 to 390 CE).

ALSO AVAILABLE

146

ALSO AVAILABLE

- Septuagint: History, Volume 2

ENOCH AND METATRON SERIES:
- Books of Enoch Collection
- Books of Enoch and Metatron Collection
- Books of Metatron Collection
- Secrets of Enoch

OTHER TRANSLATIONS:
- Apocalypses of Ezra
- Arabic Maccabees
- Hebrew Maccabees
- Life of Adam and Eve
- Memories of the New Kingdom
- Septuagint's Esther and the Vetus Latina Esther
- Septuagint's Ezekiel and the Ba'al Cycle
- Septuagint's Job and the Testament of Job
- Septuagint's Proverbs and the Wisdom of Amenemope
- The Amarna Letters
- Testaments of the Patriarchs Collection
- Tobit and Ahikar
- Ugaritic Texts: Ba'al Cycle
- Wisdom of Ahikar

www.ingramcontent.com/pod-product-compliance
Lightning Source LLC
Chambersburg PA
CBHW061805120626
46550CB00005B/2148